WOMEN'S HEBREW POETRY ON AMERICAN SHORES

POEMS BY
ANNE KLEIMAN AND
ANNABELLE FARMELANT

TRANSLATED BY
ADRIANA X. JACOBS AND
YOSEFA RAZ

EDITED BY
SHACHAR PINSKER

WAYNE STATE UNIVERSITY PRESS
DETROIT

© 2016 by Wayne State University Press, Detroit, Michigan 48201.
All rights reserved. No part of this book may be reproduced
without formal permission. Manufactured in the United States of America.

20 19 18 17 16   5 4 3 2 1

Library of Congress Cataloging Number: 2015954826

ISBN 978-0-8143-4136-0 (paperback); ISBN 978-0-8143-4137-7 (ebook)

∞

Designed by Bryce Schimanski
Typeset by Westchester Publishing Services
Composed in Adobe Caslon Pro

WOMEN'S HEBREW POETRY
ON AMERICAN SHORES

CONTENTS

Acknowledgments ix

Introduction: "Meager Gifts" from "Desert Islands"—
American-Born Women and Hebrew Poetry 1
SHACHAR PINSKER

POEMS BY ANNE (CHANA) KLEIMAN
Translated and with Notes by Yosefa Raz

Translator's Preface 17

Droplets
    Spring 23
    The Spring 25
    Again, Spring 27
    In the Straits 29
    Seas and Wind 31
    Candles Burn 33
    Behold 35
    To the San Francisco Delegates 37
    Yizkor/In Memoriam 39
    Toward the Light 41
    From the Mountaintops 43
    "I saw them in hiding" 45
    I Only Heard Your Voice 47
    To Dr. Nissan Touroff 49
    On the Threshold of the Midrasha 51
    Be Not Afraid 53

What Can I Give to You?   55
"Suddenly, you have become dear to me"   57
My Longings   59
To Lake Michigan   61
To the Musician   63
"In the motionless heavens"   65
"Today, I wept a great deal—"   67
"And always, but always, a hidden hand"   69
"Now, just as last year"   71
"I know not wherefore"   73
"And all is pained"   75
"Last night you placed your hand on mine"   77
"Now I wander lonely"   79
When Will You Come?   81
Your Eyes   83
This Is Another Dream   85
You   87
Cease and Desist   89
I Want to Die   91

ON ANDA PINKERFELD AND HER POETRY
by Anne (Chana) Kleiman

Translated and with Introduction and Notes by Shachar Pinsker   95

POEMS BY ANNABELLE (CHANA) FARMELANT
Translated and with Notes by Adriana X. Jacobs

Translator's Preface   103

Selections from *Desert Islands*

Desert Islands   111
Moment   113
"The Unwed Maiden"   115
A Song of Autumn   117
New Moon   119
Skyscraper   121
Blinding Light   123
When Europe Died   125
American Trip: A Dramatic Poem   129
Return to Zion for Your Spirit   139
The Israeli Parrot   141
Lullaby   143
Renewal   145
In the World's Heart   147

The World Is Like a Poem   149
Builder   151
Everyone Agrees   153
Far to Near   155
Cycles for Moshe, My Father Z"L   157
Farewell, Love   159
Shira Aviva   161
Job   163
Change, No Change   165
Eros   167

Selections from *Flowers of Identity*

Sad Roots   171
ID   173
Flowers of Identity   177
The Wall   179
The Circus   181
Revenge in Nature   183
Jacob and Autolycus   185
Jealousy   187
Narcissus   189
Confession   191
A Riddle   193
The Bee's Kiss   195
Two Muses   197
Bridges   199
Blurred Lines   201
Race to the Star   203
Kite   205
For a Bird   207

Notes   209

ACKNOWLEDGMENTS

First and foremost, we are grateful to Adina Kleiman and her family for sparking the idea for this project and for their support through its duration. Several years ago Adina approached Yosefa Raz with the idea of translating Hebrew poems by her mother, Anne (Chana) Kleiman. Through the poems' translation into English, she thought she would gain a better understanding of her mother's work and be able to share it with the rest of the family. Later Adina approached Shachar Pinsker to study the poems and give a lecture about Kleiman in the context of American Hebrew literature on the occasion of the first reading of the translations, which took place in October 2006 at Northwestern University. These early engagements with Kleiman's work encouraged us to think about creating this volume. We're only sorry that Anne Kleiman, z"l, did not see this project to fruition; however she was able to attend the reading and lecture and to see some of Yosefa Raz's translations in print. We also extend our deep gratitude to Annabelle (Chana) Farmelant for taking the time to meet with us on many occasions to discuss her poetry and her experiences as a mid-twentieth-century American Hebrew poet.

We thank Michael Weingrad, Alan Mintz, and Wendy Zierler for their support for the project at various stages and invaluable comments on the manuscript. Yosefa Raz extends special thanks to Maria Melendez Kelson, Chana Kronfeld, and Allan Kensky, whose insightful comments on the drafts of the Kleiman translations helped reveal their light. Adriana X. Jacobs is particularly grateful to Michael Walek for sharing his insights on Farmelant's biography and to Asya Graf and Eran Tzelgov for their very careful and critical readings of the Farmelant translations at an early stage. Shachar Pinsker would like to thank Deborah Dash Moore, Anita Norich, and the fellows of the Frankel

ACKNOWLEDGMENTS

Institute for Advanced Judaic Studies during the academic year 2013–14, which was dedicated to the topic of Jews and gender.

We are also grateful to the organizers and participants of the seminar "Locating Gender in Modern Jewish Literature" (Association for Jewish Studies, Boston, December 15–17, 2014), where Shachar Pinsker's introduction was first presented, and of the colloquium "Rediscovering America: New Scholarship on American Hebrew Literature and Its Impact on the Study of Modern Jewish Literature" (Jewish Theological Seminary, New York, December 4, 2011), where Adriana X. Jacobs spoke on Farmelant. The archival research for this project was extensive: thanks go to the staff of the Gnazim Institute in Tel Aviv and the Spertus Institute for Jewish Learning and Leadership in Chicago, as well as to Mattie Taormina at Stanford University's Special Collections, for making crucial materials available to us.

Funding from the Hadassah-Brandeis Institute at Brandeis University and the Institute for Research on Women and Gender at the University of Michigan supported this project from beginning to end. A Diller travel grant from UC Berkeley supported Yosefa Raz's archival and translation work.

Working with Wayne State University Press has been a wonderful and rewarding experience. Special thanks to editor-in-chief Kathryn Wildfong, who believed in this project and made sure everything about the publication of this bilingual volume went smoothly. Thanks to Kristin Harpster and Mindy Brown for the copyediting and production of the volume, and to Amit Ben-Yehuda for his professional production of the Hebrew version of the poems.

Yosefa Raz's translations of Kleiman's "In the Depths" (which appears in this volume as "In the Straits") and "Seas and Wind" appeared (in slightly modified form) in *Bridges: A Jewish Feminist Journal* 12, no. 1 (2007): 80–89. An earlier version of "To the San Francisco Delegates" appeared in *Bridges* 12, no. 2 (2007): 70–73. Adriana X. Jacobs's translations of Farmelant's "Skyscraper," "Desert Islands," "Renewal," "Far to Near," and "The Unwed Maiden" first appeared in her article "Hebrew on a Desert Island: The Case of Annabelle Farmelant," *Studies in American Jewish Literature* 34, no. 1, special issue, ed. Kathryn Hellerstein and Maeera Shreiber (Spring 2015): 154–74. Some of the materials in Shachar Pinsker's introduction first appeared in *American Jewish History* 79, no. 2 (2013): 182–86.

Work on this volume spanned the better part of a decade. It is the culmination of a project that was collaborative from the very beginning, and the three of us are grateful for each other's help, dedication, and generosity.

And last, but not least, we thank our families.

—Adriana X. Jacobs, Shachar Pinsker, and Yosefa Raz

Introduction: "Meager Gifts" from "Desert Islands"

American-Born Women and Hebrew Poetry

SHACHAR PINSKER

I

This volume seeks to fill a significant gap in Jewish American literature and Hebrew literature. In 2003 Alan Mintz wrote that "the existence of a substantial body of Hebrew literature written on American shores is one of the best-kept secrets of Jewish American cultural history."[1] A decade later it seems that the secret of Hebrew literature in America has been revealed. In the last few years, many articles and three new scholarly books on American Hebrew literature have been published.[2] With this renewed interest and abundance of new materials, the story of American Hebrew literature is finally getting some of the attention it truly deserves. Nevertheless, there is a substantial lacuna in this field, which has to do with the presence of women writers in this literary and cultural endeavor.

Hebrew literature in America was written and read by a small minority of Jews, and yet Daniel Persky, a prominent Hebrew writer and journalist, counted in 1927 (the height of the movement) no fewer than 110 active writers of Hebrew in America.[3] So where were the women writers in this number? After all, it was precisely in the 1920s and 1930s that women began to be active in Hebrew literature, mostly in poetry, in Europe and Palestine, as well as in Yiddish literature in America and Europe (and even Palestine). Indeed, until very recently scholars assumed that American Hebrew literature, which flourished between the 1900s and 1960s, had been the exclusive domain of East European immigrant men, as well as very few American-born writers (also men). But this common assumption is wrong. There is a small but significant body of Hebrew poetry written by American women that is yet to be read, explored, published, and studied. This volume hopes to address this lacuna and introduce two of these writers and their work.

As far as we know, Claire (Chaya) Levy was the first woman to publish a book of Hebrew poetry in America: *Kisufim* (*Longings*) in New York, in 1941. Levy was born in Grodno, Lithuania, in 1915. She was a rabbi's daughter who received Hebrew and Jewish education in the European *Tarbut gymnasium* in Grodno.[4] She immigrated to America with her family in 1928. Some of her early poems were published in Vilna, but most appeared in American Hebrew publications like *Ha-Do'ar* and *Niv*, as well as in Europe and Palestine. But apart from Levy, whose work deserves some serious scholarly work, there were two American-born women who wrote and published Hebrew poetry between the mid-1930s and the early 1960s: Anne (Chana) Kleiman and Annabelle (Chana) Farmelant, whose poems and essays are published here in the original Hebrew and in English translations by Yosefa Raz and Adriana X. Jacobs.

Anne Kleiman (née Shanin), who died in 2011 at the age of 101, was the first American-born Jewish woman to publish poems in Hebrew. Kleiman was born in 1909 in St. Joseph, Missouri, to Russian immigrant parents. As a child and adolescent during the 1910s and 1920s, she received an extensive Hebrew education at the Talmud Torah, a five-days-a-week supplemental school in St. Joseph, where she proved herself an avid and gifted student. At the age of nineteen, Kleiman moved to Chicago to study both at the University of Chicago and the Hebrew Midrasha (College of Jewish Studies). With Hebrew as the exclusive language of instruction, she studied Jewish history, rabbinic thought, Bible, Hebrew language and grammar, and modern Hebrew literature. Moshe Zalesky, a prominent Hebraist teacher and later the head of Cincinnati's Bureau of Jewish Education for a quarter-century, became her first husband. In the 1930s and 1940s, Kleiman wrote and published Hebrew poems in the Midrasha's journals as well as in the journal *Niv*. Most of these poems were collected and published in 1947, by the Chicago College of Jewish Studies and the Jewish Publication Society, as a book titled *Netafim* (*Droplets*). Kleiman also contributed to a 1950 Hebrew anthology for students, edited by Shlomo Marenoff and Moshe Zalesky. She created an adaptation of Hayim Nahman

Bialik's "The Legends of Three and Four," with the title *Shlomo u-vat hamelech* ("Solomon and the Princess").⁵ As far as we know, Kleiman did not publish Hebrew poetry after 1950—a few unpublished manuscripts exist—but she remained active in Hebrew education until her retirement in the 1970s. She was involved in various Jewish adult education activities for many more years.

A second American-born Hebrew poet, Annabelle Farmelant, currently lives in New York City. Farmelant was born to immigrant parents in Boston around 1926. Raised in Boston, she attended public schools as well as Prozdor, a Hebrew high school program of the Hebrew College. Farmelant studied at the Hebrew College in Boston and, like Kleiman, was inspired and encouraged by Hebraist teachers, notably Eisig Silberschlag. Since the 1940s, while she studied and worked as a Hebrew and Jewish educator (she also spent some time in Israel in the 1950s), Farmelant wrote a substantial body of Hebrew verse, which she began publishing in journals such as *Niv* in America and *Gilyonot* and *Gazit* in Israel, as well as in two volumes of verse. Farmelant's first book, *Iyyim bodedim* (*Desert Islands*), was issued by Kiryat Sefer in Jerusalem (1960), followed by a second volume, *Pirchei zehut* (*Flowers of Identity*), also published by Kiryat Sefer (1961). During the years in which these volumes were published, she lived in Tel Aviv, but soon after the publication of her second book, she moved back to America and settled in New York City. Since the mid-1960s, Farmelant has published Hebrew poetry very rarely; she wrote two plays in Hebrew and several in English that were never published or performed.

How can we contend with these virtually unknown women and their body of Hebrew writing? How can we begin to read, understand, and recover their poetic voices and worlds? In undertaking this endeavor we are confronted, once again, with some of the dilemmas feminist critics in France and in the Anglo-American world tackled in the 1970s, as well as those which scholars of gender and Jewish literature dealt with in the 1980s and 1990s.

Perhaps the most familiar but still extremely difficult dilemma is: Should we read these two poets—and their bodies of work—as different as they are from each other, under the rubric of "women's literature," assuming that their femininity makes these works distinct from the dominant literature written by male Hebrew writers, both in America and in Israel? Does their femininity immediately entail some connection to other women writers, in Hebrew as well as in other languages and literatures (American and others)?

After all, the poetry of Kleiman and Farmelant covers a large range of themes, moods, and styles. It touches in a powerful and moving way on their private lives and loves. It depicts the American world of vast, open nature (see

Kleiman's "To Lake Michigan"), as well as the urban space of metropolitan centers like Boston, New York, and Chicago (see Farmelant's "Skyscraper" and "American Trip"). Their poems deal with the Holocaust (Kleiman's "Yizkor/In Memoriam"; Farmelant's "When Europe Died"), the State of Israel, and public affairs in the Jewish and non-Jewish worlds. They often comment on the historical period in which they lived and wrote. Some of their poems are restless and acerbic; other are reflective and introspective. Many poems show considerable storminess (Kleiman's "Seas and Wind," "To the San Francisco Delegates"; Farmelant's "The Israeli Parrot"), in which the poets seek, and mostly do not find, a basis for idealism and stable values. And yet the gender of the two poets was surely meaningful to the way the poetry was written, read, and understood (or misunderstood).

In pondering these questions, we would do well to start with the volume *Gender and Text in Modern Hebrew and Yiddish Literature* from 1992.[6] In the introduction to this path-breaking volume, Anita Norich has urged us to examine "the ways in which the feminine as a social construct is rendered into the female as an articulating presence."[7] This is an excellent vantage point for my own inquiry. Dan Miron has famously asked in the same volume: "Why was there no women's poetry in Hebrew before 1920?"[8] Kathryn Hellerstein has examined the ways in which women who wrote Yiddish poetry struggled with, and found innovative ways to deal with, a dualism between the "Ikh" and "Zikh": the poetic "I" and the "self" in their poems.[9]

Following these and many other scholars who contributed to what is now a large body of studies on gender and Jewish literature informed by feminist theories and insights, I attempt to explain why there were so few women writing Hebrew in America, and what conditions enabled—or hindered—writing and publishing books such as the ones issued by Kleiman and Farmelant. Instead of trying to conform their works to some essential notion of "women's writing," I believe it is more productive to attend to the specific conditions of these two women writing Hebrew in mid-twentieth-century America. Thus in the following pages I will try to deal, in a necessarily succinct manner, with questions of influence, reception, and audience, as well as to explore the sexual/textual politics that are part of the poetic projects of Kleiman and Farmelant, by contextualizing a few poems from their small but significant oeuvre.

II

The first questions I would like to consider are: Why was there no published poetry written by women in Hebrew before 1936 in America, and what enabled the appearance of the poetry of Farmelant and Kleiman? Why was there so little of it in the period between 1940 and the 1960s? How was this poetry received by the dominant literary establishment in America and elsewhere? Before I try to present some answers, it is important to note that, although only three American women—Levy, Kleiman, and Farmelant—published books of Hebrew poetry, there were a number of women who wrote and published individual poems but did not bring out books. We are still waiting for future scholars to give us a fuller picture, but my own unsystematic inquiry uncovered other forgotten women, such as Yehudit Rosenbaum, Chana Gilby, Yonina Frektor, Dvora Solomon, and Rachel Lev, who published Hebrew poetry between 1936 and the mid-1960s.[10]

Going back to the questions I just posed, the first crucial fact to know about Hebrew literature in America during the first half of the twentieth century is that it was, in the words of Eisig Silberschlag, "first and foremost . . . a literature of immigrants"[11] who came to America from Eastern Europe during the mass migrations that took place between the 1880s and the 1920s. These Jewish immigrants who wrote Hebrew poetry (and later prose as well) were also educators who taught in the Jewish schools and Hebrew colleges that many of them founded, led, and nurtured for years.[12]

American-born Jewish women like Kleiman and Farmelant could not have become Hebrew poets were they not educated in these institutions. Their Hebraic world was shaped by the often intoxicating love affair with Hebrew that was the hallmark of Hebraist poets-educators like A. H. Friedlander, Shimon Halkin, Eisig Silberschlag, Moshe Zalesky, and Shlomo Marenoff, who were the teachers of these women poets in high schools and in Boston and Chicago colleges. The depth and breadth of the Hebrew education Kleiman and Farmelant received, as well as the resolute commitment to Hebrew as a core of Jewish spiritual wellspring, were quite astonishing. This explains, at least partly, why they chose to express themselves in Hebrew (and not in English).[13] This explains also a number of dominant elements in the poetry of Kleiman and Farmelant. Kleiman explicitly dedicated poems to the male Hebraist writer-educators. The title of Farmelant's first book, *Iyyim bodedim* (*Desert Islands* or *Solitary Islands*), is in dialogue with Silberschlag's first book, *Bi-shvilim bodedim* (*On Solitary Paths*, 1931), and a number of her poems establish intertextual links with poems by these American Hebraists.

However, the male-dominated Hebraic world of East European Jewish immigrants represented a double-edged sword for these women writers. The same figures who gave Farmelant, Kleiman, and other American women Hebrew education and access to its riches were also precluding them from writing and especially from publishing Hebrew poetry. The poetry written in America by Hebrew and Jewish educators followed the models set by Bialik and Shaul Tchernichovsky in the early twentieth century. Bialik, in particular, was the father figure for the American Hebrew writers. In his recent book, Alan Mintz claimed that American Hebrew poets "saw themselves in the autobiographical persona developed in Bialik's poetry: the banishment from nature, the benightedness of the *heder*, the world of faith shaken to its core, loneliness in love."[14]

For Kleiman and Farmelant, Bialik was arguably both a father and grandfather figure, and thus it is fascinating to see how, for example, Kleiman adapted Bialik's work for American Jewish students of Hebrew, as well as the ways in which both poets alluded to and wrestled with the poetry of Bialik and his American disciples. The fact that Bialik's poetic system continued to be the dominant model in American Hebrew poetry well into the 1950s was surely a problem for the women—a force to be reckoned with (even though the second part of Kleiman's book reckons with her foremothers).[15]

In his aforementioned study of the rise of Hebrew women's poetry in Palestine during the 1920s, Miron claimed that, during the first decades of the twentieth century, Bialik's lyrical poetics had crystalized as a system of thematic, generic, stylistic, and formal norms. Among the fundamental rules of this poetic system (which was the chief influence on American Hebrew poetry) were: (a) the poem must relay a private, personal experience as if it also contained national/universal content, and (b) the poem must present a rich, dense, multi-layered expression, springing from a literary culture of great depth and resonance. Failure to comply with both criteria assured immediate rejection. This, according to Miron, was one of the principal roots of the difficulty facing Hebrew women's poetry at the beginning of the century in Europe and in Palestine. Of course, Hebrew poetry was familiar with classical uses of feminine figures as collective symbols: the Jewish mother as the nation, the *shekhinah*, the muse of national poetry; the daughter of Israel, innocent and modest, embodying the purity of the national psyche. The literature of the period almost entirely lacks representation of the "new Hebrew woman," while the life of the young man is presented as a metonymy of the collective Jewish experience—a national symbolic drama par excellence.[16] Here there are obvious parallels between the predicament of Hebrew women poets in America in the 1940s and 1950s and in Palestine of the 1920s and 1930s, but there are also important differences.

A good example of the complexity of this situation can be found in the poetic relationship between Silberschlag and Farmelant. I have already mentioned the fact that the title of Farmelant's first book seems to be in dialogue with

Silberschlag's first poetry book. Silberschlag's book is a collection of ecstatic love poems, most of them focused on the romantic correspondence between nature and the female object of desire. But the book actually begins with a surprising sequence of seventeen short poems titled "*Shirei na'arah*" ("Songs of a Young Woman"), in which the speaker is the beloved of an unseen man who has dressed her in silk and installed her in a palace, where she awaits him and sings of their love. In these poems Silberschlag ventriloquizes the voice of a woman.[17] This act of ventriloquizing brings to mind poems by Bialik, Tchernichovsky, Ya'akov Fichman, and Ya'akov Shteinberg, in which these male poets adopt female voices; but in fact these are no more than masculine self-images, constructed by means of the individual poet's projection onto an imagined woman.

This posed a serious problem and a clear obstacle for women who were educated in Hebrew. These women were highly dedicated to the language; moreover, as Farmelant attested in a recent interview Adriana X. Jacobs and I conducted with her, they felt not only that Hebrew was close to their hearts but that it also came to them naturally as a language of literary expression. However, when they wanted to express themselves poetically as the subjects rather than the objects of masculine desire, a metonymy for the nation, or a projection of masculine self-images, it became a difficult, if not almost impossible, task. I believe that this goes a long way to explain why American women did not write and publish in Hebrew until the mid-1930s, why there were so few of them, and also how their poetry—once written and published—was received.

When Claire (Chaya) Levy's poems were published in a book, they were recognized mainly for the singularity of the "phenomenon" of a woman writing Hebrew poetry in America. As one of the male Hebraists, H. L. Gordon, puts it in his introduction to the volume: "The volume of poems *Kisufim* is singular and unique. It contains the longing of a young American poetess. This is the first time in the history of Hebrew literature that a volume of poetry written by a woman was published in America." He writes that "*nevoney ha-shira*" (those who understand poetry) began to notice the name Chaya Levy when she published: "A special grace was spread over her poems, the reverberations of a broken heart and the yearnings of the soul."[18] What was emphasized here, apart from the "astonishing" fact that a woman had mastered Hebrew, was the "grace," the "charm," and the "melancholic spirit" of her poetry,[19] which shows very well how a woman in America was expected (if she was) to write Hebrew poetry.

As far as I know, Levy was the only woman published in *Ha-Do'ar* and other journals edited by American Hebraists such as Menachem Ribalow and Hillel Bavli until 1936.[20] The interwar years were a time of expansion and growth for

American Hebrew literature, but these were also years of conservatism and gatekeeping. Ribalow, as editor of *Ha-Do'ar, Sefer Hashanah* (*The American Hebrew Yearbook*), and other publications, served as the chief gatekeeper for what constituted "proper" Hebraic taste.[21] It is little wonder that American-born Jewish women did not, and probably could not, publish in *Ha-Do'ar* during these years, and perhaps in subsequent years as well.[22]

III

If there was a decisive moment of change in Hebrew literature in America, at least when it comes to women, it was in 1936, the year the journal *Niv* was established. *Niv* was created to give voice to the poetry, prose, and essays of young Hebrew writers, and was issued by Histadrut ha-Noar ha-Ivri (the Hebrew Youth Organization). It was published for twenty years, with different degrees of regularity. (The journal was resurrected in 1956 and published intermittently until 1966.) *Niv* signaled a generational shift that introduced fresh energies to Hebrew literature and culture in America, which happened just at the same time that American Jews (and American Jewish writers) were turning more and more to English. From the time of their founding, the Hebrew Youth Organization and the journal *Niv* were led by a group of American-born students who served as the journal's editors, including Moshe Davis, Gershon Cohen, Eliezer Friedland, and Haim Lifshitz. Some of the literary works that appeared in *Niv* were written by young immigrant writers such as the poet Gabriel Preil, but most were by American-born Hebrew writers. *Niv* was also the journal in which many women published their poetic work, and it was the only Hebrew venue that featured women from its first issue. It is thus hardly surprising that Kleiman published in *Niv* in 1940 and Farmelant in the 1950s.[23]

This does not mean, however, that it was easy for these women to write literature or to publish a book of poetry, nor does it mean that, when a work was finally published, it was received and understood properly. This can be seen in the introduction that Shlomo Marenoff—one of Kleiman's teachers—wrote to the volume *Netafim* when it appeared in 1947:

> The poetess Chana Kleiman entered the orchard [*pardes*] of Hebrew literature with no harm [*be-shalom;* lit., in peace], and in her basket [*tene*] are these poems like first fruits [*bikkurim*], and on her lips a modest prayer, "and I am very poor." Anyone who kept an eye on her stride on the paths of poetry in the last decade would be able to testify that

from her first steps she walked up the ladder of maturity. It is true, her rhymes are few and short, but she would create wholesome and simple tunes that are pleasing to the literary ear. . . . The poetess, who lives in Chicago, is a native of the United States, and the first one among the daughters of the Midwest who knows how to pour words of lyrical supplication [*tkhines*] in the language of the fathers, which she loves "without bounds."[24]

Thus even a sympathetic and encouraging figure like Marenoff assumes that, for a young woman, entering the field of Hebrew literature is a dangerous matter. Using the Mishnaic language of "entering the orchard" (Hagiga 2:2), Marenoff portrayed Kleiman's achievement as trespassing the forbidden domain, with the author emerging out of it without being harmed. Continuing with the conceit of the orchard, he described the poems as first fruits, as "modest prayer" and "lyrical supplication" composed not in Yiddish or English but in Hebrew, "the language of the fathers."

Of course, we see here a dynamic that is very familiar, resembling the earlier reception of Hebrew poetry written by women in Palestine—including Rachel (Bluwstein), Esther Raab, and Anda Pinkerfeld—whose poetic work was "largely overlooked, often misconstrued, and consequently, subjected to cultural forgetting."[25] In a similar way the expectation was that Hebrew poetry by American women would be "modest" and "poor," and when one looks at the titles of Kleiman's and Farmelant's collections (*Droplets, Desert Islands, Flowers of Identity*), one can see the "minor key" in which Hebrew women poets have written.[26] Indeed, it makes sense that, because Kleiman and Farmelant chose to write in "the language of the fathers," in an American Hebrew poetic context that was hardly open to their innovations, they turned to the "mothers and sisters," the female poets of Europe and Palestine. Kleiman in fact was particularly captivated by Rachel (Bluwstein) and Anda Pinkerfeld, the latter of whom she met during a visit to Palestine in 1937. Later on the two women corresponded, and Kleiman even wrote a pioneering essay about Pinkerfeld's poetry (which was reconstructed from Kleiman's fragments and is published for the first time in this volume) at a time when it was hardly recognized and badly misconstrued.

However, precisely because of this affinity, it is fascinating to see how Kleiman and Farmelant dealt with these Hebrew poetic "mothers" (and "fathers") in their poetry. Probably the clearest example of this in Kleiman's work appears in the poem "*Ma eten lachem?*" ("What Can I Give to You?" 1947).

INTRODUCTION

WHAT CAN I GIVE TO YOU?

Anne (Chana) Kleiman
(Translated by Yosefa Raz)

What can I give to you
when I am but very meager?
I did not get my fill of learning
and the paths of the world are strange to me.
Only the forefathers' fire is kindled inside me
and I love my people boundlessly.

Yes, I can string together an easy tune,
to chase after winds,
to skip on the rocks,
to seclude myself with the shades of the night,
to pose riddles to the stars,
to put a tired sun to sleep, and greet
a smiling crescent moon.
Only these and one more:
I have made sorrow my companion.

What can I give to you
when I am but very meager?

This poem alludes to and engages with the famous 1926 poem *"El artsi"* (To My Country), by Rachel (Bluwstein):

TO MY COUNTRY

Rachel (Bluwstein)
(Translated by Robert Friend)

I have not sung you, my country,
not brought glory to your name
with the great deeds of a hero
or the spoils a battle yields.
But on the shores of the Jordan
my hands have planted a tree,

and my feet have made a pathway
through your fields.

Modest are the gifts I bring you.
I know this, mother.
Modest, I know, the offerings
of your daughter:
Only an outburst of song
on a day when the light flares up,
only a silent tear
for your poverty.[27]

The similarity between the two poems is apparent, and it is clear that Kleiman looked to Rachel (Bluwstein) as a source of inspiration and for an alternative model of Hebrew poetry. However the two poems are also very different. As many scholars have indicated, Rachel's poem, like her other poems and many poems by women in Palestine, deals with a female subject's difficulty in articulating her relationship with the land—the Zionist territory—that was time and again depicted as a wife, beloved woman, or mother.[28] Thus Rachel's speaker describes herself as a daughter who cannot offer much to her mother-country, neither heroic songs nor the loot of the battlefield. What she can offer instead is the "modest" or "meager" gifts of planting a tree, and of her feet making a pathway through the motherland. But the modest gift is also the very "song" or poem that she writes, which presents an alternative modernist poetics of "poverty" or minimalism that challenges maximalist poetic trends.

Kleiman's "modest" poem is not addressed to the motherland—the Zionist territory of Palestine—because it is not very relevant to her as an American writer. Instead she speaks to unmarked, second-person-plural addressees: *lachem* ("to you"). She engages—or rather challenges—this collective, which might as well be the very community of Hebrew readers and writers in America (and beyond) who might read her but also expect her to be modest, because she did not "get [her] fill of learning" and "the paths of the world are strange" to her. Kleiman clearly marks what is *different* about herself as a woman poet. Although she had a robust Hebrew and Jewish education, she did not receive the traditional Jewish *heder* and *yeshiva* education, which was seen as required knowledge for writing Hebrew literature. She was *not* an immigrant from Eastern Europe like most Hebrew writers in America and Palestine. As an American-born woman, she claims to possess within her the "forefathers' fire," perhaps as a

Jewish parallel to the Greek mythological story of Prometheus, who stole the fire from the father-god Zeus.

What Kleiman's speaker can offer to the community of readers is seemingly just "an easy tune," something that appears to be a subcanonical kind of poetry. However, this *zemer* is one that can "pose riddles to the stars," "put a tired sun to sleep," "greet a smiling crescent moon." This can be read as a different poetic relationship with nature, one that enables the speaker to express her joy and her sorrow but, in contradistinction to the Bialik and American Hebraists, in a non-romantic poetic system. When, after all this, we read the last two lines (which repeat the first two)—"What can I give to you? / when I am but very meager?"—this utterance acquires an ironic, subversive tone, which was completely lost on readers like Marenoff.

Almost a decade later, when Farmelant wrote and published her poetry, the situation had changed somewhat. In addition to publishing her poems in the American *Niv*, she appeared in the Israeli journals *Gazit* and *Gilyonot*, which were edited by Hebrew writers and editors (like Yitzhak Lamdan) who were interested in young American writers. But the sexual/textual politics that characterizes many of Kleiman's poems manifests itself in a different yet parallel way in Farmelant's poetry as well. A small but instructive example of this can be found in the poem "*Ha-'almah she-lo hitchatnah*" ("The Unwed Maiden"), published in the volume *Iyyim bodedim*.

"THE UNWED MAIDEN"

Annabelle (Chana) Farmelant
(Translated by Adriana X. Jacobs)

after a poem by Sappho

"On the twig above
an apple reddens."
The maiden's nest rests
on the lower step;
The women buzz
like bees in the company of men.
Still virgin after the vintage and oil harvest—
Among these thousands of gatherers
not one was able to pluck you?

What is remarkable, even strange, about this poem is that the title and the first two lines are presented as quotations, and the poem is marked as being written "after a poem by Sappho." Anyone familiar with the fragments of Sappho's lyrical poetry would indeed recognize the poem Farmelant evokes. But a closer reading reveals that the title is not Sappho's title, that the quote is not exactly a quote, and that Farmelant's intertextual dialogue in this poem is really with (at least) two poets. The poem clearly draws on fragment 105a, one of the most famous fragments attributed to Sappho:

as the sweetapple reddens on a high branch
high on the highest branch and the applepickers forgot—
no, not forgot: were unable to reach.[29]

Sappho's fragment is untitled, so Farmelant's title—"The Unwed Maiden"—is an invented, intriguing one. Likewise, what she presents in quotation marks as what might be a Hebrew rendering of the fragment is far from a simple act of translation.[30] Both the title and the (mis)translation, though, show Farmelant's creative appropriation of Sappho as an alternative "poetic mother," mixing it with that of the Hebrew "(grand)father," Bialik. The title might in fact "solve" a problem in reading Sappho's fragment. As Jack Winkler tells us, archaic lyric poems, such as those composed by Sappho, were intended not for private reading but for public performance before an audience.[31] This fragment, which describes a late-picked apple, was most likely part of a song recited at a wedding. Thus the simile of the reddened apple supposedly refers to a bride. But there is a problem in the poem: if the apple-pickers have overlooked the apple, or couldn't reach it, then the woman who is presumably the "sweetapple" is not wed, or was not wed until this point. If the apple is "ripe" but unattainable, it might mean that, even after marriage, the maiden would remain secure from her husband's appropriation. This is probably why Farmelant calls the poem "The Unwed Maiden," a title with a double meaning, which mirrors the double meaning of Sappho's fragment.

As Winkler tells us, the real "secret" of Sappho's erotic simile of the unreachable apple on the highest tree branch is an image not only of the bride's sexual organ but of women's sexuality and consciousness in general. Sappho knows this "secret" in herself and in other women, and she celebrates it in her poetry, as does Farmelant in her Hebrew verse. But Farmelant's creative (mis)translation of Sappho goes further, because she steals the language of the (grand)father and appropriates it in order to present a female subjectivity and female sexuality in Hebrew. Like stealing the forefathers' fire? When Farmelant's speaker uses the Hebrew words *zalzal* (twig) and *ken* (nest), every Hebrew reader would identify allusions to Bialik's poetry, especially the poems "*Tzanach lo zalzal*" ("A Twig Fell," 1911) and "*Hachnisini tachat knafech*" ("Bring Me in Under Your Wing," 1905). These celebrated poems confirmed Bialik's masterful use of multiple historical layers of Hebrew and solidified his poetic system, but also exposed fissures in his subjectivity and his problematic concept of femininity and female sexuality.[32] By appropriating Bialik (and his American Hebrew followers), and putting "his" words together with Sappho's exploration of female sexuality, Farmelant creates a potent and potentially subversive hybrid in Hebrew.

As Adriana X. Jacobs has suggested in a recent article about Farmelant, this poem can also be read, at least retrospectively, as "a critique of the sexual politics and problems of reception that shaped—and constrained—the development of American Hebrew poetry in general, and Farmelant's poetry in particular."[33] Farmelant's poetry (and Kleiman's as well) remained that apple that "not one was able to pluck," also because it was "unreachable," because very few wanted to or could reach it, read it, and understand it.

This volume is an invitation to readers to take the first step toward what was, for far too long, unreachable.

POEMS BY ANNE (CHANA) KLEIMAN

Translated and with Notes by Yosefa Raz

Translator's Preface

Anne (Chana) Kleiman, the humble and simple Midwestern "daughter" who entered the orchard of poetry unscathed, carrying a basket of first fruits,[1] was an old woman and a grandmother when I met her in 2007, at the first reading of these translations in Chicago. I remember her sitting in the front row, wearing white gloves. Her hands shook a little, but she smiled and listened intently. The room was filled to capacity with family and friends, attesting to Kleiman's rootedness in her community; though at the same time this emphasized how strange it was to have to translate the poems of such a deeply rooted local poet.

I am so curious how the older Anne might have rewritten her exuberant, exultant poem "I Want to Die" as she entered the "orchard" of old age. I wonder if there could be a poem that could celebrate her long life and love of Hebrew poetry, marked by her translation of youth into age, English-speaking life into Hebrew poetry, and back again into my English. I confess to a feeling of loss in reading and translating these poems—I wanted to read more poems by Kleiman about maturing love, becoming a mother, a grandmother, a teacher. What would the fierce prophetic poet of "Seas and Wind" write about the State of Israel, the Cold War, Vietnam, her own American Hebraist life? How would she react to Adrienne Rich, Anne Sexton, Sylvia Plath?

As opposed to many of the American Hebraists writing in the 1930s and 1940s, Kleiman was American born, and English was her mother tongue. So why, then, Hebrew? Undoubtedly, Kleiman felt an unusually strong connection and identification with Hebrew. In "What Can I Give to You?" she writes, "the forefathers' fire is kindled inside me / and I love my people boundlessly." I believe that Hebrew created greater imaginative possibilities for Kleiman, while at the same time it came to impose limitations and finally silence.

By adopting the prophetic voice made famous by Bialik and even, at times, speaking in the male voice, Kleiman could declaim with fierce authority on messianism, injustice, genocide, the formation of the United Nations, and the destiny of the Jewish people. Perhaps a Jewish American woman writing in English would be expected to be more sweet or genteel. At the same time, Hebrew narrowed her audience and influence. It's almost as if the poetry of H. N. Bialik and Rachel (Bluwstein), Anda Pinkerfeld, and Leah Goldberg created an imaginative horizon for Kleiman, a made-up Hebrew landscape (which could include Lake Michigan!), beyond which the words could not travel. Her favorite song was a musical arrangement of Rachel's poem "And Perhaps These Things Never Were," an apt anthem for the land of this Hebrew-American poetry.

My work on these poems began with an invitation from Adina Kleiman, Anne's daughter, who told me she had a manuscript for me to translate that was written in *Ivrit shel Shabbat,* fancy, or "Sabbath Hebrew." At that time I did not know that Hebrew poetry, especially in its grand prophetic tones, would become central to my own intellectual life. I grew into the poems over the course of my graduate studies, and my appreciation for Kleiman's use of the Hebrew echo-chamber grew. My translation method, too, evolved. I began by trying to smooth out what seemed like rough, unidiomatic edges—the extra "ands" of biblical Hebrew, the high language, the formal imagery. I substituted contemporary American expressions, contractions. However, a translation workshop with Chana Kronfeld at UC Berkeley encouraged me not to try to domesticate Kleiman's Hebrew. Instead, I tried to recreate the way Kleiman's biblical and rabbinic intertextual allusions were woven into modern Hebrew, creating a "Sabbath Hebrew." I found that the best way to capture this effect in English was to utilize the vocabulary and rhythm of the King James Bible, its "shall"s and "behold"s, its "wither"s and "Let him kiss me with the kisses of his mouth" from the Song of Songs.

While, in the later part of the book, the poetry claims to be "meager" or "simple," we need also to remember the tone of fierce demands, such as the poem dedicated to the Hebraist youth: "Let us have a census today in the camp! / Let us expel the corpses among us / and we will know: /who is for us / and how to seize the reins." In fact, the poems vacillate between a grand prophetic maximalism and a more melancholic, lyrical minimalism. The grand prophetic tone of the poetry allows the speaker to imagine herself cresting the waves of the

Portrait of Anna (Chana) Kleiman, Chicago, 1937.

biblical Song of the Sea in "Seas and Wind" or hanging on to the ends of the earth with "mutinous nails" to demand God's attention ("In the Straits"). Though Kleiman cites extensively from Isaiah, Jeremiah, and Ezekiel, she also alludes to female prophetic figures—Miriam and Deborah—suggesting the possibility of a female prophetic-poet. In my favorite poem, "My Longings," which mixes language from Isaiah, Bialik, and Goldberg, Kleiman is able to strike a balance between the prophetic and the lyrical, imagining sharing a blessing of "light beams" with her female interlocutor, who can also "slake [her] thirst with their radiance." Thus the poet rewrites the traditional language of the *shekhinah*, filtered through Bialik's erotic address to a female lover, into a poem of female friendship.

Droplets (1947)[1]

אביב

אֲהַבְתִּיו, עֵת עַל חַלּוֹנִי יְכַרְכְּרוּ
בִּמְשׁוּבַת הַחֶדְוָה,
צִיצֵי עָלִים, גַּלְגַּלֵּי אוֹרוֹת וְצִפְרִירִים
זַכִּים—רַכִּים—
וְהוּא בְּתוֹכָם.
יְקַפְּצוּ, יְדַלְּגוּ, יִתְהוֹלְלוּ
יָד בְּיָד,
הָלְאָה—הָלְאָה, מַטָּה—מָעְלָה,
יְרַפְרְפוּ, יִצְחֲקוּ,
לֹא יָנוּחוּ, לֹא יַחְדְּלוּ,
עַל חַלּוֹנִי.

אֲהַבְתִּיו, עֵת בֵּין פְּעָמַי
לִי יְחַיֵּךְ מִסְּגַל־חֵן,
וּבְכֶסֶף צְלִילֵי הַצִּיּוּץ
יְקַדְּמֵנִי לְשָׁלוֹם;
עֵת הָרוּחַ שְׂעָרַי יִפְרֹם
וְרֶגַע יִשְׁקֹט
נִכְלָם, תָּמִים,
נֶחְבָּא אֶל עֲשָׂבִים.
אֲהַבְתִּיו, הָאָבִיב!

Spring

I love him[2] when tiny leaves,
wheels of light, and zephyrs[3]
dance in exultant breezes on my window
pure—soft—
and he is inside them.
They jump, skip, cavort,
hand in hand,
more—more, up—down,[4]
flutter and laugh,
do not rest, do not stop
on my window.

I love him, when he smiles at me:
a sweet violet between my footsteps,
when he greets me
with silvery birdsong;
when the wind musses my hair
then for a moment rests.
Bashful, innocent, hiding among the grasses.[5]
I love him, oh the Spring!

הָאָבִיב

הַבֹּקֶר אֶת עִקְבוֹת הָאָבִיב מָצָאתִי,
כָּךְ—בִּשְׁגָגָה.
אַט אַט צָעַד, וּפְעָמָיו כֹּה זָעִיר.
חֶרֶשׁ בֵּין שְׁלוּלִיּוֹת הִתְפַּהֵק, הִתְנַעֵר—
וַיֵּחָבֵא.

אָנֹכִי בְּדַרְכִּי, אֶת עִקְבוֹתָיו גִּלִּיתִי,
וָאֲשַׁחֵר לוֹ.
דּוֹמֵם מְצָאתִיו, לֹא הֵהִין
עֵינַיִם צוֹחֲקוֹת אֵלַי שָׁמַיִם תּוֹעִים הֵרִים,
וַיֵּחָבֵא. בְּתוֹכְכֵהוּ הִתְעַטֵּף.
אַךְ קוֹלוֹ לוֹחֵשׁ: אָבוֹאָה, בּוֹא אָבוֹא!

The Spring

This morning I found the footsteps of Spring[6]
just so—unintentionally.
He tread slow and easy;
and his step was so slight.
Hushed between the puddles
he yawned to himself, shook himself off—
and he hid.

I, on my way, I discovered his footsteps
and lay in waiting.
I found him still, he did not dare
lift his laughing eyes toward the wayward sky.
And he hid. He wrapped himself inward.[7]
But his voice whispers:
I shall come, indeed I shall come!

ושוב אביב

וְשׁוּב אָבִיב.
מִתְכַּחֲלִים שָׁמַי
וּמִשְׁתּוֹבְבִים צַפְרִירִים בִּמְשׁוּבַת עֲדָנִים.
בְּפַעֲמֵי תִּינוֹקוֹת יְרַקְּדוּ עַל תֵּבֵל דַּנַּי,
וִילַטְּפוּ, וִילַטְּפוּ, וְיִלְאֲטוּ וְיָרֹנּוּ . . .

אָז בּוֹקֵעַ וְעוֹלֶה
הֵד הַמָּחָר.
מִתְּהוֹמַי יִתְפָּרֵץ וְנֶאֱכַל בִּמְשׁוּבָה,
וּפִיו יְדוֹבֵב: . . .
" . . . אוּלַי . . . "

אוּלַי זֶהוּ הַמְבַשֵּׂר!
אוּלַי אֵלֶּה פְּעָמָיו . . . !
כִּי אֵיכָכָה תָּרֹן תֵּבֵל בַּאֲבִיבָהּ
וֵאלֹהִים בּוֹ לֹא יִצְהַל,
וְלֵב אָדָם לִקְרָאתוֹ לֹא יִכְלֶה?

הִשְׁתּוֹבְבוּ צַפְרִירַי,
גִּילוּ, צַהֲלוּ וָרֹנּוּ.
וְיִשְׁמַע אָדָם,
וְיִזְכֹּר אֱנוֹשׁ, וְיֵדַע כִּי—
שׁוּב אָבִיב.

Again, Spring

Again, spring.
My skies dip themselves in blue.
and zephyrs[8] misbehave in truant pleasure.
They dance with baby steps on the sorrowing world,
and they caress, and they caress, and they whisper and rejoice . . .

Then the echo of tomorrow
breaks forth and rises.
From my depths it bursts, and is consumed,
its mouth urges: . . .
". . . perhaps . . ."

Perhaps this is the herald![9]
Perhaps these are his footsteps . . . !
>   For how can the world delight in its spring
>   and God shall not cry out for joy within?[10]
>   and the heart of man[11] shall not longingly respond?

Whirl up my zephyrs,
exalt, rejoice, and sing.
And man shall hear,
and mortal shall be mindful,[12] and know—
spring again.

במיצר

אוֹי לִי כִּי נִדְמֵיתִי . . .
אֵין מָנוֹס
מִשֵּׁנִי הַזַּעַם שֶׁעָטוּ עָלַי כְּכִידוֹנִים.
אֵין מִפְלָט
מִשּׁוֹטֵי מַשְׂטֵמָה מַצְלִיפִים,
מִתְהוֹלְלִים בִּמְחוֹל שִׁגְעוֹנָם.
וַאֲנִי נוֹעֵץ צִפָּרְנֵי־מֶרֶד בַּשְּׁחָקִים
וְזוֹעֵק מָרָה לָרוּחוֹת.

אוֹי לִי, אִמִּי, כִּי יְלִדְתִּינִי
לְעִתּוֹת מְצוּקָה וְעָמָל.
בְּהִתְבַּרְזֵל הַדָּם
וּבֶאֱרֹב נֶפֶשׁ לְנֶפֶשׁ.
כִּי חָדְלוּ פְרָזוֹן, אָרְחוֹת מִישׁוֹר חָרֵבוּ,
וְעֵינַיִם מִתְנַכְּלוֹת מוֹשְׁכוֹת בִּצְחוֹקָן
אֶל הַתֹּהוּ.

אִי, מְנַחֲמֵי הַהֶבֶל! מֵאַגָּדוֹת־שָׁוְא נִלְאֵיתִי
וּלְשִׁירֵי עַרְשְׂכֶם הָרָדוּם לֹא אוּכַל.
לֹא אֶבְנֶה מִגְדָּלִים עֲלֵי לַעַ הַר־גַּעַשׁ,
לֹא אָקִים הֵיכְלֵי־שֵׁן עַל פִּי־תְהוֹם.
הַאֶסְחַף? הַאֶחְדַּל?
הַאֲמִין אִם אַשְׁמִיל בִּישִׁימוֹן הָעִתִּים,
וְעַמּוּד הֶעָנָן הֵן כְּבָר סָר,
הֵן כְּבָר סָר . . . ?

In the Straits[13]

Woe is me for I am undone . . .[14]
No escape
from the raging teeth that came upon me like spears.
No refuge
from the lacerating whips of hate,
frenzied in their mad dance.
And I affix[15] my mutinous nails into the skies
and shout bitter to the winds.

Woe is me, my mother, for you bore me
in days of distress and toil.[16]
When blood turns to iron[17]
and when soul waits to prey on soul,
for the rulers have ceased to rule,
and the level ways are ruined,[18]
and hostile eyes pull with their laughter
into chaos.

Fie, vain comforters! I have grown weary of futile fairytales
and cannot be lulled to sleep with your cradlesongs.
I will not build towers on the maw of a volcano,
I will not erect ivory palaces on the brink of the abyss.
Shall I be swept away? Will this be my end?
Shall I go leftward or rightward in the wasteland of these times,
and the pillar of cloud is already gone,
is it already gone . . . ?[19]

ימים ורוח

אֶת כָּל הָרוּחוֹת בִּי עָצַרְתִּי
וָאָרִיצֵם: פּוּצוּ, אַחַי, הִתְרוֹצֲצוּ
וְטַלְטְלוּנִי לַמֶּרְחַקִּים
אֱלֵי קְצֵי קִצִּים שׁוֹמֵמִים
אֶל גְּדוֹת יַמִּים גּוֹעֲשִׁים.
אַחַת אֱהִי עִמָּהֶם
לְבָן רוֹתֵחַ
מֶרֶד שׁוֹצֵף.

גְּאֵה גְּאוּ, יַמִּים, וְאָנֹכִי בְּתוֹכְכֶם.
זַעֲקוּ וְצַוְּחוּ, וְאָנֹכִי בְּרֹאשְׁכֶם.
זְרוֹעוֹתַי לְעָנְקֵי מִשְׁבָּרִים תִּתְכַּנַּפְנָה,
בְּסִפֵּי תֵבֵל נֹאחַז
נְעַזְעֵם וּנְחַלְחֲלֵם
עַד יֵהוֹם בַּשְּׁחָקִים הֵד חֶרְדָּתָם.

הִקּוֹמוּ, וְהַצְלִיפוּ, וְשַׁסְּעוּ סִפֵּי עוֹלָם!
גַּעֲשׁוּ וְרִקּוּ בְּכָל מְרִי מֶרְיְכֶם
וְתִתְחַלְחַל תֵּבֵל, וְנִרְתְּעָה לְאָחוֹר
וְתִתְפַּלֵּץ בַּעֲווֹנוֹתֶיהָ,
וְתֵאָכֵל בְּרִשְׁעָהּ!

Seas and Wind

I corked up all the winds inside me
and then I let them run: scatter,[20] my brothers,
go hither and thither,
and bear me to the distances
to the desolate ends of ends
to the shores of tempest-torn seas.
I will be one[21] with them
boiling whiteness
surging mutiny.

> Seas, whirl up gloriously,[22] and I shall be within you.
> Cry out and rage, and I shall be at your crest.
> My arms will be winged into waves,
> we will grip the ends of the world,
> we will shake them, make them tremble
> Until the echo of their terror roars in the heavens.

Arise, and whip, and split open the ends of the world!
Storm and spew out the bitter might of your revolt
and the earth shall shudder, driven back,[23]
and it shall reel in its sins
and be consumed in its evildoing![24]

נֵרוֹת דוֹלְקִים

נֵרוֹת דוֹלְקִים עַל יָמִים שֶׁמֵּתוּ
יָמִים צוֹחֲקִים.
הִתְלַקְּחָה נִשְׁמָתָם,
וְדָעֲכָה.

גָּעֲשׁוּ הַיָּמִים
הָמוּ מְאֹד.
הִתְפַּלְּצוּ
וְנִתְּקוּ

עַל כֵּן
לֹא שָׁלְווּ הַתְּמוֹלִים
שַׁבַּת עוֹלָמִים לֹא מָצָאוּ.
עוֹד זוֹעֵק הַדָּם
עוֹד נוֹהִים נְעוּרִים נֻתָּקוּ.

נֵרוֹת דוֹלְקִים עַל יָמִים שֶׁמֵּתוּ

Candles Burn

Candles burn for days that died[25]
laughing days.
Their souls blazed,
and were extinguished.

The days stormed
howled mightily.
Shuddered,
and were undone.

Therefore
the yesterdays[26] were not tranquil
they did not find eternal rest.[27]
The blood still cries out
The youth that was severed still wails.

Candles burn for days that died

הַבִּיטָה

הָאֵל,
אֵלֶיךָ קָרָאתִי—
הַבִּיטָה כַּמָּה לְשִׁמְךָ יוֹם יוֹם מַתַּי,
הַבִּיטָה!
וּמַדּוּעַ אֶת עֵינֶיךָ הֶעֱלַמְתָּ?
הַאֶת צֶלֶם בָּנֶיךָ, אַתָּה בְרָאתָם,
יָרֵאתָ?

הָאֵל,
בְּךָ נִשְׁבַּעְתִּי,
וְאַף כִּי שֶׁבַע אֶסָּחֵף, לֹא אָמוּת.
אֶת כָּל סִפֵּי שָׁמֶיךָ אֲזַעְזֵעַ,
אֶת כָּל אֲמוֹתֵיהֶם בְּכַפַּי אֶעֱקֹר
עַד אֵלֶיךָ אָבוֹאָה,
וְשָׁמַעְתָּ.

Behold[28]

God,[29]
    It is you I call to—
    See how much I die for your name day by day,
    Behold!
    And why have you averted your eyes?
    Do you fear to face the likeness[30] of your own created sons?

God,
    I swear to you,
    and though I be swept away sevenfold, I will not die.
    I will rattle the farthest reaches of your skies,
    I will tear out its pillars with my fingers,
    until I reach you,
    and you shall listen.

לְמִקְרָאֵי סן פרנציסקו

דְּבָרַי אֲלֵיכֶם, מְחוֹקְקֵי חֻקּוֹת תֵּבֵל!

בְּבוֹא הַיּוֹם, עֵת
יִנְהַר אֶל הַהֵיכָל כָּל שׁוֹחֵר שָׁלוֹם,
וִידַעְתֶּם, כִּי בְּטֶרֶם בּוֹאֲכֶם
וְהַבַּיִת מָלֵא—
אַף יִרְעֲדוּ הַמְזוּזוֹת מֵהָמוֹן.
שְׁלִיחֵי־אֱמוֹת נֶאֱמָנִים הֵמָּה—

אֲשֶׁר אָב וּפֶה לָנוּ הָיָה,
כָּרַע, נָפַל—
אֲשֶׁר בֵּן הָיָה, וְגִבּוֹר הָיָה,
וְנִקְרַב—
אֲשֶׁר אָהוּב הָיָה, וְחַי הָיָה,
כָּל נוֹפֵל בְּטָהֳרָה עַל אַרְצוֹ
כָּל הַמֵּת עַל קְדֻשַּׁת תּוֹרָתוֹ . . .

שְׁלִיחִים נֶאֱמָנִים הֵמָּה, שְׁלִיחֵי־הָאֱמוֹת.
וְהִקְשַׁבְתֶּם!
כִּי לָהֶם הַיָּד, וְלָהֶם כָּל מוֹשָׁב בַּיּוֹם הַהוּא!
וּרְאִיתֶם!
וִידַעְתֶּם!

To the San Francisco Delegates[31]

My words to you, lawmakers of the world![32]

    When the day comes,
    when the seekers of peace shall flow unto the assembly-hall,[33]
and you shall know, even before your arrival
the house will be filled—
even the doorposts will quake with the crowds.[34]
They are the loyal delegates of the nations:—

    Who was a father and a mouth to us,
        fell down, died—
    Who was a son, and a hero,
        sacrificed—
    Who was beloved, who was alive,
    all who fell, pure, for their country
    all who died for holiness of their torah . . .[35]

They are loyal messengers, delegates of the nations.
    And you shall listen!
    For theirs is the power, and every seat in the house shall be theirs on
        that day![36]
    And you shall behold!
And you shall know!

יזכור

וַאֲנִי, אָנָה אֲנִי בָא . . . ?
כִּי —
קָמוּ הַתְּמוֹלִים וְנִצְּבוּ:
נֶעֱרָפִים
נִשְׂרָפִים
נֶחֱנָקִים
נִקְבָּרִים חַיִּים.
נִתְקַבְּצוּ לְמִנְיָנָם, עֲטוּפֵי טַלִּיּוֹת־אֵשׁ
וְקַדִּישׁ אִלֵּם יְמַלְמְלוּ
עַל מִקְדָּשׁ וְיַבְנֶה נֶחֱרָבִים.

וַאֲנִי, אָנָה אֲנִי בָא . . . ?

Yizkor/In Memoriam

And I, whither shall I go . . . ?[37]
    because—
        the yesterdays rose up and stood at attention,
            beheaded
            burned
            choked
            buried alive.
They gather for their prayer,
a quorum wrapped in prayer shawls of fire,
and murmur a mute *kaddish*[38]
for the temple and the remnant at Yavneh, all destroyed.[39]

And I, whither shall I go . . . ?

לקראת האור

למסיימים

אָמַרְנוּ:
בְּמִשְׁעוֹל הַדּוֹרוֹת נַעְפִּיל, לֹא נֵט
אֵשׁ אָבוֹת בְּחֵבֵנוּ נִצֹּר.
אָזְנֵינוּ אָטַמְנוּ לְלַעֲגֵי מַה־לָּכֶם,
וַנָּבוֹז לְשֹׁאֲנַנֵּי־חִדָּלוֹן.

אֶת אֱלֹהֵי הַבְּלִימָה שָׂרִינוּ,—וַנּוּכַל . . .

וְרָאֹה:
עַל כָּל שִׂיא צוֹפִים כְּבָר הַצַּגּוּ,
מְבַשְּׂרִים,—עַל רֹאשׁ כָּל פִּסְגָּה;
הַמַּחֲנֶה הִתְקַדֵּשׁ—וַיֶּחֱרַץ
לִקְרַאת הַשַּׁחַר הַבּוֹקֵעַ . . .

Toward the Light

for the graduates

Thus we declared:
> We shall climb the path of generations, shall not stumble.
> We shall kindle the fire of our fathers in our breasts.
> We have shut our ears against the mockery of why-bother,
> and we scorn those blithe to destruction.
>
> We've striven with the gods of nil,[40]—and prevailed . . .

and behold,
> sentries have already been posted on every peak,
> heralds,—on every mountaintop;
> the assembly has sanctified itself—and hastens
> toward the breaking of the dawn . . .[41]

מראשי השיאים

לרב ש. גולדמן

הַסָּכַּתְּ! מֵרָאשֵׁי הַשִּׂיאִים מִתְפּוֹצֵץ הַקּוֹל,
קוֹל הַלֶּהָבוֹת:
"הָהּ, בָּנִים מְסֻכָּנִים!
מֵחַטֵּט בָּאַשְׁפָּתוֹת
קוּמוּ, הָקוּמוּ!
הָעִירוּ, הָעוֹרוּ!
לִבְשׁוּ עֹז! הִתְעוֹדָדוּ!
לְכוּ וְנֵלְכָה
לְבִצּוּר מִקְדָּשֵׁנוּ!"

מִי הַקּוֹרֵא?
אֵיזֶהוּ הַקּוֹל?

אָכֵן, יְדַעְתִּיו,
הֵן זָכוֹר אֶזְכְּרֶנּוּ
מִמְּחִלּוֹת אֶתְמוֹלִי
בּוֹקֵעַ הֵד —
מַשָּׂא הַכַּרְמֶל . . .
חֲזוֹן הָעֲצָמוֹת . . .

אָכֵן, רְאִיתִיו
שָׂעֲרוּ לִרְוָחוֹת
בְּרַק עֵינָיו לַמֶּרְחָק
וְלִבָּבוֹ —
לַשְּׁחָקִים.

From the Mountaintops

to Rabbi S. Goldman[42]

Take heed![43] The voice blasts from the mountaintops,[44]
the voice of flames:
> "Ah, poor children!
> Arise, get up
> from rummaging in the gutters!
> Awake and be stirred!
> Gird yourself in strength! Take heart!
> Come let us go
> fortify our Temple!"[45]

>> Who is calling?
>> What is that voice?

Oh yes, I do know it.
I do earnestly remember it still.[46]
Out from the trenches of my yesterdays
the echo resounds—
the oracle at Carmel . . .[47]
the vision of the dry bones . . .[48]

Indeed, I did behold him
his hair flying in the winds
his eyes sparking to the distance
and his heart—
soaring to the skies.

POEMS BY ANNE (CHANA) KLEIMAN

* * *

לנוער העברי

בַּמַחֲבוֹאִים
רְאִיתִים יוֹשְׁבִים "שִׁבְעָה"
עַל בָּנִים חַיִּים־מֵתִים.
בִּיגוֹנָם יִמַּקּוּ
וְאַחַת יְדוֹבְבוּ:
"אָבְדוּ."

כֹּה יָשְׁבוּ בָּדָד
יַסְפִּידוּ בָּנִים
דַּם עֲקִיבָאוֹת בְּעוֹרְקֵיהֶם יִזְרַם.
בָּנִים,
בְּשִׂפְתוֹתֵיהֶם "קָדְשָׁה" יְמַלְמְלוּ
וּבְיוֹם תְּשׁוּאָה לָהֶם
הֵיכַל אֱלֹהִים יְטָשׁוּ.

וְלֹא יָדַעְתִּי
מַה יַּעֲשֶׂה עוֹד לִבְנֵיהֶם
וְלֹא נַעֲשָׂה בָּם?
הֵן מִשְׁפַּע אַהֲבָה
יָרְדוּ לַדֶּחִי.

וְעַתָּה—
עַד אָנָה נְהַלֵּךְ עֲטוּיֵי אֵימִים
וְקַדִּישׁ שָׁחוֹר מְרַחֵף עַל רָאשֵׁינוּ
הֵן בְּיָדֵינוּ חֹמֶר הַמָּחָר
וְלֹא נֵדַע קָרְצֵהוּ?
וַאֲנִי אָמְרִי לָכֶם:
מִפְקָד הַיּוֹם בַּמַּחֲנֶה!
נִפְלִיט פְּגָרִים מִקִּרְבֵּנוּ,
וְנֵדְעָה:
מִי לָנוּ
וְאֵיכָכָה בַּהֶגֶה נֹאחַז.

* * *

for the Hebraist Youth

I saw them in hiding
sitting "*shiva*"
for dead-alive children.
They rot in their grief,
and all at once, they murmur,
"they are gone."

Thus they sit solitary,[49]
eulogize children
the blood of Akiva coursing through their veins.[50]
Children,
their lips mumble "*kedusha*"[51]
but on the day of their laudation
they will abandon the hall of God.[52]

And I did not know—
what else can be done for their children
that has not been done?
For an excess of love
has sunk them low.

And now—
>how long will we walk about, garbed in terror
>a black *kaddish* hovering over our heads?
>For we hold in our hands the clay of tomorrow
>do we not know how to form it?

>Here is my word to you:
>Let us have a census today in the camp!
>Let us expel the corpses among us
>and we will know:
>who is for us
>and how to seize the reins.[53]

רק קוֹלְךָ שָׁמַעְתִּי

לְזֵכֶר ח.א. פרידלאנד ז"ל

פָּנִים לֹא הִכַּרְתִּיךָ,
אַף יָדְךָ לֹא לָחַצְתִּי;
רַק קוֹלְךָ שָׁמַעְתִּי
וָאֶבֶן רַז שֶׁפַע מְבָרְכֶיךָ.

עוֹד אֶזְכֹּר:
עֵת כָּל קָשֶׁה-יוֹם עֲמוּס-תְּלָאָה וָמַר-רוּחַ
חָרֵד לְמָחָר הַלְאֹם וְדוֹרֵשׁ אֱלֹהַּ;
עֵת אַלְפֵי עֵינַיִם שׁוֹאֲלוֹת:
מַה יֶּהִי?

וּמֵעַל לָרֶטֶן מְהַסְּסִים וְרֶטֶט לְבָבוֹת
"לָאו" שֶׁל יִשְׂרָאֵל מְרַחֵף בֶּחָלָל—
אָז קוֹלְךָ שָׁמַעְתִּי, אַתָּה הַשָּׁלֵו בַּנְּבוֹכִים.
וָאֵדַע: לֹא אַתָּה זֶה הַמְדַבֵּר;
כִּי רֵיחַ הַלַּיְלָךְ וְצִיּוּץ הַקִּיכְלִי
וְאֹדֶם שְׁקִיעָה בְּיוֹם עָיֵף
וְצִפֳּרִירִים מְרַטְּטִים בֵּין עֳפָאִים,
וּצְחוֹק תִּינוֹק, וְאַנְקַת אֵם
סֵבֶל אֱנוֹשׁ וִיגוֹן אֻמָּה.

אָכֵן יָדַעְתִּי, עֵת הָאֱלֹהִים
נִשְׁמַת הַשַּׁבָּת לָאָדָם הָאֱצִיל לַיּוֹם,
עָלֶיךָ הֶעֱנִיק פִּי שִׁבְעָה—
עַל כֵּן תָּרֹן בְּךָ הַנְּשָׁמָה הַיְתֵרָה
וְשַׁחַר בּוֹקֵעַ תֶּחֱזֶה בְּלֵיל עֲרָפֶל.

I Only Heard Your Voice

In memory of A. H. Friedland, of blessed memory[54]

I did not know your face,
I did not even shake your hand;
I only heard your voice
and understood the secret of the multitudes who praised you.

More, I remember:
When the downtrodden, burdened with struggle, and bitter in spirit
fear for the nation's future, seek their God;
when thousands of eyes ask:
what will be?

And above the grumbles of the hesitant and the trembling of hearts
this "Whither"[55] of Israel hovering in the air—
then I heard your voice, you, the serene among the perplexed.[56]
and I knew: it's not *you* speaking;
but the fragrance of the lilac and the song of the thrush
the crimson of the sunset on a weary day,
and zephyrs[57] trembling in the branches,
and the laughter of a baby, a mother's keening;
the suffering of man and the grief of a nation.

So I know, at the moment God
bestowed a Sabbath soul for one day on man,[58]
he gave sevenfold to you—
therefore the second soul sings in you:
you have seen the breaking of the dawn
in the night dark with fog.

POEMS BY ANNE (CHANA) KLEIMAN

לד״ר ניסן טורוב

שי

אַשְׁרֶיךָ, רַבִּי, אֲשֶׁר הֶאֱצִיל עָלֶיךָ הָאֵל
רוּחַ, וְעֹדֶן וְחֶדְוָה,
וַאֲשֶׁר מִבֵּין עַפְעַפֶּיךָ, צְנוּעוֹת
יִצְטַחֲקוּ נְעוּרִים וְתִקְוָה.

To Dr. Nissan Touroff[59]

an offering

Happy are you,[60] my teacher, as the Lord granted you
gentleness, and refinement and joy;
Between your modest eyelids,
youth and hope make merry.

על סף המדרשה

ליובל העשרים

מֵאָז אָל בֵּין כְּתָלַיִךְ נִכְנַסְתִּי
יָדַעְתִּי תּוֹחָלָה וָעֹז
בְּיָדַיִךְ נֶאֱמָנוֹת רֻקַּעְתִּי
רָקוֹעַ וְלִבוּשׁ מַסֶּכֶת אָבוֹת
וְרוּחַ הַמָּחָר בִּי נֻפַּח.

אַתְּ לִי עֶרֶשׂ נְעוּרִים, בָּךְ גָּדַלְתִּי
בַּחֲלַל חֲדָרַיִךְ עוֹד נִשָּׂא צְלִיל צְחוֹקִי תָּמִים:
קַלּוּ רַגְלַי אָז בְּסַחַרְחֹרֶת הַמָּחוֹל
וְהֵד זִמְרָתִי אַף יַעֲנוּ הַסִּפִּים.

וּבַמַּחְשַׁכִּים, עֵת יֶחֱרַד הַלֵּב
וְכָל עַיִן לַתֹּהוּ צוֹפָה,
אַתְּ לִי מִקְלָט מִסַּעֲרוֹת הַיּוֹם,
אֵלַיִךְ אָבוֹאָה,
בִּלְטִיפָה אַחַת אֶתְחַזֵּק, אֶתְאַזֵּר,
אֵדַע שׁוּב אֱמוּנִי עֲדֵי־עַד.

On the Threshold of the Midrasha[61]

for a 20th anniversary

Since I entered within your walls
I have known hope and strength;
your hands fashioned me faithful
intertwined into the ancestors' warp and weft[62]
and the breath of tomorrow was blown into me.[63]

For me, you are a childhood lullaby. I grew inside you.
My innocent laughter still peals within your halls.
My feet were then light with the giddiness of the dance
and even the doorframes echoed my melody.

And in the darkness, when the heart grows scared
and all eyes look toward chaos[64]
you are my refuge from the day's storms,
I shall come to you,
and with a single caress, be strengthened, fortified,
know again eternal fealty.

אל דאגה

לשלמה מראה־נוף, בהערצה

אַל דְּאָגָה! וְכֹה לֶחָי!
קָדִימָה צַעֲדוּ
אַל הֶרֶף, אַל דִּי!
מַה מוֹקֵשׁ לָנוּ,
מַה לָּנוּ מִכְשׁוֹל?
אִם אַךְ נַחְפְּצָה
יָכוֹל נוּכַל!
כֹּה בָּנוּ אַחֵינוּ
כֹּה אָנוּ נִבְנֶה,
אַל יִפֹּל כָּל רוּחַ
אַל יֵאוּשׁ בַּפֶּה!
כֵּן, הָבוּ כָּל שְׁכֶם
וְכָל יָד תְּנוּ,
הַמָּחָר לָנוּ נָקִימָה
וְאַל תִּדְאָגוּ!

Be Not Afraid

To Shlomo Marenoff, in admiration[65]

Be not afraid! And take heart![66]
March on,
do not falter, do not stop!
What can hinder us,
What be a stumbling block?
If we only will it,
we can do it!
Thus our brothers built,
thus we shall build.
Let no spirit falter,[67]
let no mouth be filled with despair.
Yes, put shoulder to shoulder,
and give an outstretched arm,
let us raise our tomorrow
and do not be afraid!

מָה אֶתֵּן לָכֶם?

מָה אֶתֵּן לָכֶם
וְאָנֹכִי דַּלּוֹתִי מְאֹד?
רֹב תּוֹרוֹת לֹא שָׂבַעְתִּי
וּשְׁבִילֵי עוֹלָם לִי זָרִים.
רַק אֵשׁ אָבוֹת בְּחֶבִּי נָצַרְתִּי
וָאֹהַב אֶת עַמִּי עַד אֵין קֵצָה.

כֵּן, זֶמֶר קַל יָדַעְתִּי שִׁיר,
לִרְדֹּף אַחֲרֵי רוּחוֹת
לְדַלֵּג עֲלֵי סְלָעִים,
לְהִתְבּוֹדֵד עִם צִלְלֵי לַיִל,
לָחוּד חִידוֹת לַכּוֹכָבִים
לְהַשְׁכִּיב שֶׁמֶשׁ עָיֵף, וּלְקַדֵּם
פְּנֵי סַהַר צוֹהֵל.
רַק זֹאת וְעוֹד אַחַת:
אֶת הַכְּאֵב הָיִיתִי לְרֵעַ.

מָה אֶתֵּן לָכֶם
וְאָנֹכִי דַּלּוֹתִי מְאֹד?

What Can I Give to You?[68]

What can I give to you
when I am but very meager?[69]
I did not get my fill of learning
and the paths of the world are strange to me.
Only the forefathers' fire is kindled inside me
and I love my people boundlessly.

Yes, I can string together an easy tune,
to chase after winds,
to skip on the rocks,
to seclude myself with the shades of the night,
to pose riddles to the stars,
to put a tired sun to sleep, and greet
a smiling crescent moon.
Only these and one more:
I have made sorrow my companion.

What can I give to you
when I am but very meager?

* * *

וּלְפֶתַע, יְקָרְתָּם לִי
שִׁבְעָתַיִם בִּי נֶחֱרַתְּתֶּם,
כִּי קָמוּ תְּמוֹלִים
אַף רָקְדוּ
עַל מָחָר שַׁכּוּל־בּוֹדֵד.

* * *

Suddenly, you have become dear to me
by sevenfold,[70] engraved in me,
for yesterdays have arisen
even danced
on my lonely, bereaved tomorrow.

גַּעְגּוּעַי

לְלֵאָה . . .

מוּל חַלּוֹנִי זַהֲרוּרִים יִצְהָלוּ
יְקַרְצוּ, יְלָאטוּ:
—קוּמִי, צְאִי—
רַב לָךְ שְׁכָב, הַדְּוִויָה,
לִבְשִׁי עֹז, וַחֲרֹגִי

אָז יִתְחַזֵּק יִצְרִי הַכּוֹאֵב
יִתְאַזֵּר לָקוּם
אַךְ אָחוֹר יִצָּנַח
חֲדַל אוֹנִים.

וְאַתְּ . . .

הֵן זַהֲרוּרַי גַּם אֶת חַלּוֹנֵךְ יִפְקְדוּ.
קוּמִי, דּוֹלְקִים אֲחוֹתִי
וְרָוִית מִזִּיוָם
וְאָצַלְתְּ גַּם לִי מִבִּרְכָתָם.

אֶל גְּדוֹת הַמִּישִׁיגָן צְאִי לָךְ
וְדִלַּגְתְּ עַל הַסְּלָעִים
דַּלֵּג וְקַפֵּץ
אַחַת לָךְ
אַחַת לִי
וְיַצְלִיפוּ הַגַּלִּים
וְיָפוּצוּ לְרַגְלַיִךְ.

שָׁם אֲרֻכּוֹת תִּתְבּוֹדְדִי
וְהִתְעַטַּפְתְּ יַמִּים וָרוּחַ . . .
וּבְרָטוֹב גּוּפֵךְ, שְׁכוּר גַּלִּים וְצָרִיחוֹת בְּנֵי־שַׁחַף
אֵלַי בּוֹאִי,
תְּכַסִּינִי בְּבִגְדֵךְ, סְפוֹג רֵיחוֹת אֲגַמִּים
וְיָדֵךְ הָרַעֲנַנָּה הַטְּלוּלָה
עַל מִצְחִי תִּסְמֹכִי . . .
וְשָׁלְוָה נַפְשִׁי.

My Longings[71]

For Leah . . .

Across from my window, light beams[72] exult,
they wink, they whisper:
arise, go forth—
You have lain too long, cheerless one,
gird yourself in strength and break free.[73]

Then my sorrowing spirit grows stronger,
braces to rise,
but falls backward
helplessly.

    and you . . .

Yes, my light beams visit your window too.
Arise, give them chase, my sister
and slake your thirst with their radiance,
and grant me too a part of their blessing.[74]

Go forth to the banks of Lake Michigan
and skip among the rocks
skip and jump
one for you
one for me
the waves will lash
and scatter at your feet.[75]

There, seclude yourself for hours,
wrapped in seas and wind . . .
and in the dampness of your body, drunk on waves and sea-gull cries,
come to me
cover me with your dress,[76] drenched in the smell of lakes,
lean your dew-fresh hand on my forehead . . .
and my soul will rest.

לַמִישִׁיגָן

לְעוֹלָמִים הָיִיתָ לִי
לְעוֹצֵר גַּעֲגוּעַי עַד.
נָסוֹגוּ מֵימֶיךָ
וְנָדַמּוּ,
וּבְדוּמִיַּת שִׁקְטָתָם
אֶת עַצְבִּי שִׁחַרְתִּי.

לְעוֹלָמִים הָיִיתָ לִי
לִמְגַלֵּה רָזַי עַד.
עֵת דִּמְדּוּמִים
אֵלֶיךָ נִכְסַפְתִּי,
וּבְשַׂחַק גַּלֶּיךָ
פִּתְרוֹנוֹת בִּקַּשְׁתִּי.

To Lake Michigan[77]

You have always been
my vessel of endless yearning.
Your waters abated,
quieted,
and in their hushed stillness
I sought my sorrow.

You have always been
my revealer of eternal mysteries.
At twilight
I longed for you
and in your tossing waves—
I wished for answers.

לַנַגָן

לֹא אֵדַע עַל מָה וְלָמָּה—
אַךְ נִקְלֶטֶת הַנְּגִינָה,
וְדוֹמַעַת בִּי הָעַיִן,
וְרוֹעֶדֶת הַנְּשָׁמָה,
וְנִכְסֶפֶת, וְעוֹרֶגֶת
נֶאֱבֶקֶת וְחוֹרֶגֶת,
וְדוֹבֶקֶת
בְּתוּגַת הַצְּלִיל.

דְּמִיתִיךָ הַנַּגָּן:
רֹאשׁ אֱלֵי כִּנּוֹר
תָּנוּעַ—
אִילָן רַךְ עַל פֶּלֶג זַךְ
מֵנִיד שִׂיאוֹ לְנַהֲמֵי הָרוּחַ.

To the Musician

I do not know when and why—
but the moment the melody takes hold,
my eyes tear,
my soul trembles,
and yearns, and longs,
wrestles and breaks free,
clings
to the melancholy of the chord.

I picture you, the musician,
head to violin
quivering—
like a sapling by a clear brook
swaying its crown to the keen of the wind.

POEMS BY ANNE (CHANA) KLEIMAN

* * *

בִּדְמִי שְׁחָקִים
אֶת הַלְּבָנָה
חָזִיתִי—

נִדְמְתָה
בְּצִיץ הָמְטִי דַמְטִי,
שׁוֹקְדָה עַל שְׁבָרֶיהָ.

* * *

    In the motionless heavens
    I saw
    the pale moon[78]—

She appeared
    a Humpty Dumpty egg,
    brooding over her fragments.

POEMS BY ANNE (CHANA) KLEIMAN

* * *

הַיּוֹם רַבּוֹת בָּכִיתִי—
צִיץ רָכִיךְ
הַבְקִיעַ
לִקְרַאת
שְׂחַק־עֲרָפֶלִים.

* * *

Today, I wept a great deal—
a tiny bud
burst
toward
the sky-fog.

* * *

וְתָמִיד, אַךְ תָּמִיד יָד נִסְתֶּרֶת
תִּפְרֹט עַל נִימֵי הַתּוּגָה.
עַל מָה כֹּה יִדְאַב הַלֵּבָב?
יְבַקֵּשׁ שָׁם אֵי־שָׁם תְּשׁוּבָה.

* * *

And always, but always, a hidden hand[79]
plaits on these strands of sorrow.
What so distresses the heart?
Let it seek there, somewhere, an answer.

POEMS BY ANNE (CHANA) KLEIMAN

* * *

כְּאָשְׁתַּקֵּד
אוֹתָהּ עֵת, אוֹתָהּ מַנְגִּינָה,
אוֹתוֹ כְּאֵב . . .
וְעוֹד לוֹטָה הַיּוֹם בָּעֲרָפֶל
וְעוֹד הַיָּד מְגַשֶּׁשֶׁת . . .

* * *

Now, just as last year:
same season, same melody,
same pain . . .
and the day still shrouded in fog
and the hand still groping . . .

POEMS BY ANNE (CHANA) KLEIMAN

* * *

אֵינִי יוֹדַעַת עַל מָה
נִצְּבוּ לְעֵינַי הַיּוֹם
כָּל תְּמוֹלַי.
סָחָבוּנִי אֲלֵיהֶם,
וַיִּרְקְדוּ
וַיִּרְמְזוּ
וַיִּבְכּוּ . . .
וָאֲלַטְּפֵם בְּיָד דּוֹאֶבֶת
וָאֲמִיצֵם בְּלֵב רַחוּם,
וָאֲשַׁלְּחֵם.—

* * *

I know not wherefore
all my yesterdays
stood before me today.
> They dragged me to them,
> and danced,
> and insinuated,
> and cried . . .

and I caressed them with a sorrowing hand,
and drew them to me with a merciful heart,
—and sent them off.

POEMS BY ANNE (CHANA) KLEIMAN

* * *

וְהַכֹּל כּוֹאֵב,
וְהַכֹּל דּוֶֹה.
כָּל תְּמוֹלַי בִּי תְּמֵהִים,
הֲהָיוּ?
כֹּה מַהֵר חָלְפוּ,
עָבְרוּ בְּלֹא יוֹדְעִים.
נֶעֶרְבוּ תּוּגָה, גִּילָה,
וַחֲלוֹמוֹת—

* * *

And all is pained,
and all grieves.
All my yesterdays wonder within me,
were they real?[80]
They passed so quickly,
went by unnoticed.
A swirl of sorrow, joy,
and dreams—

POEMS BY ANNE (CHANA) KLEIMAN

* * *

אֶמֶשׁ יָדְךָ עַל יָדִי סָמַכְתָּ
וַתָּנַח לָהּ אֲרֻכּוֹת כֹּה קְצָרוֹת.
וָאֶחֱשֹׁב: הֲתִזְכֹּר זֹאת בַּיָּמִים הַבָּאִים?
הַאֶרְאֶה מָחָר בְּעֵינֶיךָ הַחֹם הָעוֹלֶה עַתָּה
מִלִּבָּבְךָ עַל יָדִי?

* * *

Last night you placed your hand on mine,
and it rested lingeringly-so-briefly.
And I thought:
will you remember this in the days to come?[81]
Will I see this warmth—
rising from your heart to my hand—
in your eyes tomorrow?

* * *

עַתָּה אָשׂוּחַ בּוֹדְדָה
בִּדְרָכִים יָדַעְנוּ שְׁנַיְנוּ,
בְּכַפַּי לְלַקֵּט חֲלוֹמוֹת
שָׁם לָרֹב זָרִינוּ . . .

* * *

Now I wander lonely
on paths we both knew,
gather the dreams
that we scattered so richly—
trying to hold them in my hands.

מתי תבוא?

כָּל הָעֵת לְךָ צִפִּיתִי.
אָמַרְתִּי: מָתַי תָּבוֹא?
וְהִנֵּה הִגִּיעוּנוּ יְמֵי סְתָו
עָלִים נוֹשְׁרִים בְּכָל דֶּרֶךְ
וְרוּחוֹת חֲדָשִׁים יְנַשֵּׁבוּ.

אֶל קְצוֹת הַמַּיִם לִי הַיּוֹם יָצָאתִי.
אֲנִי אֶצְבְּעוֹתַי הוֹשַׁטְתִּי—וְהִנְּךָ
אֶת יָדִי לָקַחְתָּ, וְיַחַד
בֵּין קֶצֶף הַגַּלִּים דִּלַּגְנוּ, וְנִרְטַבְנוּ.
כֹּה צָחַקְנוּ . . .
פְּרוּמֵי שֵׂעָר הִתְכּוֹפַפְנוּ וּבָרַחְנוּ
אֲנִי לְפָנֶיךָ, אַתָּה אַחֲרַי.
רֶגַע פָּנַי הֲסִבֹּתִי—
וְאֵינְךָ—

עַד אָנָה כֹּה אוֹסִיף
בּוֹדֵדָה הֲלוֹךְ?
אַתָּה עַמִּי וְלֹא אִתִּי,
מָתַי תָּבוֹא?

When Will You Come?

All that season, I waited for you.
Wondered: when will you come?
And now, our autumn has arrived
leaves fall on every path,
and new winds blow.

Today I went to the water's edge.
I reached out my fingers—you
were with me, took my hand, and together
we skipped among the waves and foam, all wet,
laughing so . . .
Wild-haired, we knelt down, then up and racing—
I was before you, you—behind me.
For a moment, I looked away—
and you were gone—

How long
must I walk lonely?
You are within me
but not with me.
    When will you come?

POEMS BY ANNE (CHANA) KLEIMAN

עֵינַיִךְ

רִאשׁוֹנוֹת
עֵת רְאִיתִיךְ, אָמַרְתִּי
עֵינַיִךְ,
אַךְ לִשְׂחוֹק נִבְרָאוּ.

וּנְשַׁקְתִּיךְ.

וְדָמְעוּ עֵינַיִךְ
וְנָפָלוּ.
וָאָבֶן, כִּי
אַךְ לִכְאֵב נוֹצָרוּ.

Your Eyes

In the beginning
When I beheld you, I said,
your eyes
were only created for laughter.[82]

and I kissed you.

Then, tears stood in your eyes,
and fell,
and I realized,
your eyes
were made but for sorrow.

זה עוד חלום

זֶה עוֹד חֲלוֹם
אַתָּה,
צְחוֹקְךָ—
הַכֹּל.

בְּעֵינֶיךָ תֶּחֱזֶה מָחָר.
אַתָּה סָח:
אֲנִי וָאַתְּ
אָנוּ יַחְדָּו,
בְּמָחָר . . .

הֲתֵדַע?
לֹא אֲצַפֶּה
לֹא אֲכַלֶּה
דַּיֵּי יוֹמִי
כִּי—
אַף הוּא
לִי עוֹד חֲלוֹם.

This Is Another Dream

This is another dream
you,
your laughter—
all this.

Your eyes see tomorrow.
You utter:
you and I
we together,
in the tomorrow . . .

    Do you know?
I do not hope
I do not long
my day today is enough
for—
even this day
is another dream.

אתה

אַתָּה שָׁזוּר בִּי
כְּנֶרֶם פְּלָגִים בְּחֵיק אֲדָמָה
כְּכָסָף גַּלִּים בְּאוֹר לְבָנָה,
אַתָּה בִּי שָׁזוּר.

אַתָּה כָּרוּךְ בִּי
כְּרֵיחַ בְּשָׂמִים בְּלֵב שׁוֹשַׁנָּה
כִּצְלִיל הַזֶּמֶר בְּחֵיק הַחוּגָה
אַתָּה בִּי כָּרוּךְ.

You

You are woven through every thread of me[83]
like the flow of streams in the midst of the earth
like the silver of waves in the light of the moon,
woven through me.

You are bound to me
like the smell of perfume in the heart of a rose
like the notes of song in the nightingale's breast
you are bound to me.

חֲדַל וָלֵךְ

חֲדַל וָלֵךְ,
טֶרֶם עַיִן בְּעַיִן תִּתָּקֵל
וְתִמְזֹגְנָה נְשָׁמוֹת
טֶרֶם לֵב בְּלֵב תִּתְכַּתֵּשׁ
וְתֹאכְלֵנוּ לֶהָבָה,
חֲדַל, וָלֵךְ.

טוֹב עַתָּה לֶכֶת,
כְּאָח וָרֵעַ תִּוָּתֵר לִי.
לֵךְ—טֶרֶם שִׁמְךָ עַל שְׂפָתַיִם יְמַלֵּל,
דְּמוּתְךָ בְּכָל הֵלֶךְ יְבֻקַּשׁ
וְקוֹלְךָ בֵּין רוּחוֹת יִנָּשֵׂא.
עַתָּה, חֲדַל, וָלֵךְ!

Cease and Desist [84]

Cease and desist
before eyes happen upon eyes
and souls merge
before heart spars with heart
and is consumed by flame.
Cease, and desist.

> Better now to leave,
> remain my friend, my brother.
> Cease—before your name scrapes the lips,
> your image is sought in every passing face,
> and your voice carries in the wind.

Now cease, and desist!

אני רוֹצָה לָמוּת

אֲנִי רוֹצָה לָמוּת
בְּעוֹד רוֹתְחִים דָּמַי בִּי
בְּעוֹד יְכַוֵּן הַגּוּ
לְכָל צַפְרִיר,
בְּעוֹד רוֹטֵט הַלֵּב
לִקְרַאת צִיּוּץ הַדְּרוֹר,
אֲנִי רוֹצָה לָמוּת.

אֲנִי רוֹצָה לָמוּת
בְּעוֹד יְחַמְּמֵנִי
גִּיל מְשׁוּבַת פְּתוֹת־שְׁלָגִים
רוֹקְדוֹת בַּסְּעָרָה,
בְּעוֹד תְּלַטֵּפְנָה אֶצְבָּעוֹת
לֹבֶן סַהַר תָּמִים,
אֲנִי רוֹצָה לָמוּת.

אֲנִי רוֹצָה לָמוּת
בְּעוֹד מָלֵא פִּי צְחוֹק יַלְדוּת
בְּעוֹד בָּאָדָם אֶתֵּן אֵמוּן
בְּעוֹד אֶדְאַב יְגוֹן אֱנוֹשׁ,
אֲנִי רוֹצָה לָמוּת.

אֲנִי רוֹצָה לָמוּת
בְּעוֹד לְלִבְּךָ תִּלְחָצֵנִי
בְּעוֹד יְשַׁכְּרֵנִי רֹךְ נְשִׁיקוֹתֶיךָ
בְּעוֹד יְלַטְּפֵנִי חֹם עֵינֶיךָ,
אֲנִי רוֹצָה לָמוּת.

I Want to Die

I want to die
while my blood still riots in me,
while the body still arches
in every breeze,
while the heart still thrills
to the chirp of the sparrow,
I want to die.

I want to die
while I can still be warmed by joy
in a flurry of snowflakes
dancing in the storm
while my fingers can still caress
moonlike whiteness,
I want to die.

I want to die
while my mouth is still full of childhood laughter
while I still trust in Man[85]
while I still suffer mortal's grief,
I want to die.

I want to die
while you still press me to your heart
while still drunk with the soft kisses of your mouth[86]
while the heat of your eyes still caresses me,
I want to die.

"ON ANDA PINKERFELD AND HER POETRY" BY ANNE (CHANA) KLEIMAN

Translated and with Introduction and Notes by Shachar Pinsker

Translator's Introduction

The following essay by Kleiman on the Hebrew poet Anda Pinkerfeld Amir (1902–82) was never published in any language. The handwritten Hebrew original was found in her personal archive. Kleiman had written it at some point in the 1940s, possibly as a draft for future publication in a journal or for a public talk. Indeed some of the materials in this article were incorporated into an English talk titled "The Jewish Woman as a Cultural Force," which Kleiman presented much later. I used materials from the English lecture to translate and fill in some gaps in the Hebrew notes. I also included some of Kleiman's own translations of key passages from Pinkerfeld's poems.

This essay is important for several reasons. It shows the extent to which Kleiman was actively reading and thinking about Hebrew poetry by women in Palestine. It makes clear that Kleiman was influenced by these women writers and that she was engaged in a dialogue with them in her own writing. Pinkerfeld was especially important for Kleiman, and the two women had a personal relationship for some time. They met when Kleiman visited Palestine in 1937, and they corresponded for some years after that visit. Reading the article, one realizes that certain characteristics which Kleiman finds in Pinkerfeld's poetry appear in her own American poetry. Thus it reveals as much about Kleiman's poetics as it does Pinkerfeld's. The article is also important because, at the time it was written, Pinkerfeld was recognized and appreciated only for her children's poetry. Her main poetic output, which was not for children, was misread and misunderstood by critics. This article by Kleiman constitutes one of the first important attempts (following the lead of Rachel [Bluwstein]) to truly understand Pinkerfeld's poetry.

"On Anda Pinkerfeld and Her Poetry"

In one of the volumes of *The American Hebrew Yearbook*, I happened to come across a *poema* [long narrative poem] titled *Geisha Lian-Tang shara* (*The Geisha Lian-Tang Sings*, 1935), by Anda Pinkerfeld. The short preface to the volume reads: "Tshang-Tu, a descendant of a royal Japanese family, read me the poems of the geisha Lian-Tang, which were addressed to one of his forefathers in the twelfth century." I was surprised. In fact I was in awe, and a bit jealous as well. It is indeed astonishing to find a Hebrew poet who can, for the first time in our literature, savor and delight in the literary cherries of Japan.

Anda Pinkerfeld started to write poetry at a very young age in Poland. Her first poems were written in Polish rather than Hebrew. However, upon her immigration to Palestine, she decided to express herself only in Hebrew. Not too long after her immigration, she published her first book of verse, *Yamim dovevim* (*Whispering Days*, 1929).[1] In this volume she proved to be a consummate artist of the short poem; there is hardly any poem in the book longer than a page.

In her early poems we see the young, emotional Anda. Nothing passes before her without making an impression. Her eyes examine and absorb everything. And how unpretentious and spare is her poetic expression. Her first published Hebrew poems are discrete impressionistic fragments, portraits of nature that cause the heart to quiver:

> Blessed be oh man
> You halted the train
> For a tiny bird
> Caught on the track.
>
> Oh Blessed be, little girl
> With your tiny hand you helped
> A giant porter carry a mighty load,
> Blessed be, in the world. (6–7)

But as one continues to read the book, the speaker is revealed in a wide variety of constantly changing dispositions and moods. We see her everywhere: restless, with windswept hair, she runs, jumps, hops, and skips hither and thither. She embraces the whole wide world—it feels so good, so good, to be alive:

> In the market square I shall whistle a piercing call
> Hold your ears, delicate ladies.
> A jolly peddler will offer me an apple
> I shall eat it, sweet and red. (22)

How content she is with her life, this young woman. Alive for a red apple! Alive for a smiling sun! Alive for life! Etc. A red apple, a smiling sun, a fresh laugh, a beautiful tune, all of these give her reasons to live; every day is precious, "as precious as gold, pure gold." In the poem "I Forgot Everything," she writes:

> My day is God's blessing:
> In the morning it rises, in the evening it sets: this sun—
> Bless it!
> Even God forgot tomorrow and yesterday,
> And the calm
> And the birds in the sky. (12)

But suddenly the little one becomes sad—the joy of life has been taken from her upon observing an old handicapped woman ("A Female Amputee Blessed Me This Morning," 23). Like most poets, she is hurt by the pain of all creatures. When such pain strikes her, she feels that all human beings are her children, and like a mother kissing the wounds of her son, she caresses and comforts all humankind: her sons, "humans—children in sleep" (8). And when she is deep in thought and contemplating her world, the Jewish world, a world of profound pain, she concludes,

> We are a sad and tired people
> Nothing hurts anymore,
> Yet all is in pain:
> Heaven, sea, earth, night, and God himself
> Hidden behind a hundred clouded veils. (60)

When sadness, pain, and sorrow are at their peak, she is overcome by a dark pessimism and decides that "God in the sky has hidden his Face" (53)—"God has no heart / No heart for humankind and his own image" (54)—and writes "A Lullaby to Sorrow" (55).

It is fascinating to see the development of Pinkerfeld's poetry in *Whispering Days,* her first book. She begins with tiny poems—the fruits of fleeting impressions—and she continues more forcefully, with "weighty" poems that stem from her experiences in *Eretz Yisrael*.

Her next published volumes of poetry, *Yuval* (1932) and *Gitit* (1937), are very different.[2] Both books open with long, biblically inspired narrative poems. Equally intriguing are her understanding and portraits of biblical figures like Yael (the wife of Heber the Kenite), Sisera (Judges 4:2), Esau, and Jephthah's daughter.

For example, she describes Sisera as a lover of Yael. In her account, Sisera, with Deborah, runs from the battlefield during the night in order to arrive at the tent of his lover. "With old and torn clothes, blood and dust cover your face" (11). Instead of handing Sisera over to his enemies (as the Book of Judges implies), Yael kills him with her own hands out of deep compassion and profound love.

In another poem Pinkerfeld depicts Esau not only as a man of the field but as a man of the spirit, a person of strong character who disdains the material properties that his brother, Jacob, attempts to take from him with deceit. In the poem about him, Esau understands that Jacob will never be able to cheat him and steal the blessing of God from him (22–24). Pinkerfeld makes a similar poetic move with the figure and story of Jephthah's daughter. She completely transforms these biblical figures, and the result is that the readers of her poems are able to see these figures through a new and different lens.

Pinkerfeld also excels in her nature poems. Her understanding of nature is so profound that it seems as if she is unified with it. In the long narrative poem "Yuval," she transforms earth into a living creature, with different moods and desires: Birds are the children of earth's laughter. In the summer, when the heat is unbearable, she talks to the ground: "crouching by your feet like a heavy mammal / a groan smothered in your chest"; and when there is a storm: "Shattered you would go out dancing / You would run riot, wild thing, / cause a storm / in your wakening dance" (10).

"I am like a straight, but not wise, tree," she writes in one poem. In another poem she goes out to play with Pan, god of Nature, because he is her lover; and they go out to play hand-in-hand: "He embraces me with his mighty grassy arms," she says, as they run off together in the rain (19–20). And when she feels intoxicated by this love of life, she calls out, bursting, overflowing.

Pinkerfeld is as successful in her erotic love poems as she is in her nature poetry. In these poems there is a mixture of pain, suffering, sensuality, and longing. The heart widens with deep understanding of the sorrow of the world and its people. One of the best examples of her love poetry is in the aforementioned volume *Geisha Lian-Tang shara*. Where can one find such exquisite simplicity?

It seems that the more you read this long poem, the more tenderness and beauty you find there. You find the mango tree, you smell its flowers; you can even taste of the heavy rice wine, the quivering of Lian-Tang's heart, longing for her lover. True poetry is here in every word.

Just as we saw her contentment with, and joyfulness of, life in the early poems, now we find her upset and concerned about historical events. She is distressed, but this doesn't help. There is no rest or shelter from the evil hand that threatened the *Yishuv* in Palestine. It seems to her that even the land itself made a covenant with the killers. With the bitterness that comes from a deep sadness, she cries for an Arab woman ("Rejoice, the Woman of Arabia"[3]), after reading in the newspaper (July 1936) about a bomb that injured eighteen people, including a woman and a four-year-old child. She is mourning, and she misses those nights—the nights of quiet and peace, when the bells of the camel caravans could be heard, those sounds that seem to point us to our common past.

We must not forget also the fact that Pinkerfeld excelled in poetry for children. For these poems alone she won the coveted Bialik Prize in children's literature (1936). In this area she has carved an eternal place for herself and will forever be etched in the hearts of the children who read her poems.

The poet Rachel (Bluwstein) wrote about Anda Pinkerfeld's "spare and the clear poetry," about her "freedom from conventions of rhyme, meter, and stanzaic form," and the "elasticity and succulence of her language."[4] Simplicity, sparseness, and lyricism—with these traits Anda Pinkerfeld acquired many friends and came to be admired by many readers of modern Hebrew poetry, wherever they happened to reside.

POEMS BY ANNABELLE (CHANA) FARMELANT

Translated and with Notes by Adriana X. Jacobs

Translator's Preface

In a poem titled "The World Is Like a Poem," the poet Annabelle (Chana) Farmelant describes the poetic text as "an unnamed wanderer / in the world's splendor." As I translated these lines from Farmelant's original Hebrew into my English, I puzzled over the implications of the metaphor. I understood wandering to mean the ways in which a poem circulates through time and place, how it is exchanged between readers, and also how it travels in and through translation. Anne Carson's observations on translation could apply to the writing of poetry itself: "You come to a place where you are standing at the edge of a word and you can see, across the gap, the other word, the word you're trying to translate, and you can't get there. And that space between the word you're at and the word you can't get to is unlike any other space in language. And something there is learned about human possibilities, in that space."[1]

But in what way is the poem "unnamed"? I thought of how translating a poem simultaneously assumes and undermines the poet's authority by replacing her textual voice with my own but at the same time acknowledges that whatever origins the original text could claim—the influences and materials that brought it into being—can no longer be claimed. It is in this respect that a poem wanders in translation, but in the context of women's writing in the 1950s and early 1960s, Farmelant's acknowledgment of the unsettled and undomesticated state of the poem also feels political. Had Farmelant continued writing, she may have entered into a more sustained dialogue with the revisionary work undertaken in the 1970s by American female poets like Adrienne Rich.[2] At the same time, for an American Hebrew poet like Farmelant, these lines also evoke the solitude and anonymity of belonging to and participating in a waning literary culture.

In early 2009 Shachar Pinsker approached me with the opportunity to translate Farmelant's work and sent me a sampler of poems that drew from her two collections, *Iyyim bodedim* (*Desert Islands*, 1960) and *Pirchei zehut* (*Flowers of Identity*, 1961), both published in Israel. The poems sparked my interest in the project and in Farmelant's work, as did the prospect of participating in the "recovery" of an unknown poet, and specifically a female poet; but the lack of context for the poems was, and still remains, disorienting. In his study of American Hebrew poetry, in a chapter aptly titled "The Last Mohicans," the scholar Michael Weingrad describes Farmelant as "a decidedly postwar sensibility, restless and often acerbic," whose poems "often seek and do not find a basis for idealism and stable values in a post-Holocaust world."[3] Weingrad had corresponded directly with Farmelant but warned me that she was not inclined to speak about her poetry in any substantive detail.[4] He sent along the last address he had on file for her, which confirmed that Farmelant lived not only in New York City but also, by a stroke of luck, in my neighborhood.

Farmelant was mystified that I was translating her work, as it had been years since she had written a poem, having dedicated most of her creative efforts to playwriting. She was familiar with Weingrad's interest in her work but was curious to know what kind of audience existed for English translations of her poems, a question that touches on the question of readership that vexed American Hebrew writers for decades. The Israeli poet Dory Manor, who has translated Charles Baudelaire and Stéphane Mallarmé into Hebrew, once told me that he avoided translating living authors because, in his words, "the dead don't argue." Though I shared his misgivings, it quickly became clear in our first meeting that Farmelant was entirely estranged from her poetry. "It's like it happened to a different person," she would say.

Farmelant was born in Boston around 1926 to Russian immigrants Morris (Moshe) and Lena (Leah), and raised there along with her younger brother.[5] She attended public schools as well as Prozdor, the Hebrew high school program of Hebrew College. She was named "Chana Biala," a name later Anglicized to "Annabelle."[6] According to Farmelant, a family friend who loved Edgar Allan Poe suggested the name to her parents, though she went by "Chana" at Hebrew College and briefly adopted the pen name "Chana Bat-Leah." Asked to describe her decision to write Hebrew poetry, Farmelant remarked, "*Ivrit modernit krova me'od la-tanakh*"—modern Hebrew is close to the Bible—and, switching back to English, she characterized Hebrew as "my language." Indeed, when pressed to describe in more detail her relationship with the Hebrew language, Farmelant noted that when she wrote poetry in Hebrew, the language came to her naturally; she could recall no difficulties in writing, nor did she discern any major difference between her Hebrew and the Israeli Hebrew of the period. Yet one need only compare Farmelant to a poet like Yehuda Amichai to observe that differences did exist. Though Amichai and Farmelant were not native Hebrew speakers, the cultural, political, and linguistic milieux in which they developed as Hebrew poets shaped remarkably distinct poetries. By the late 1940s, when Farmelant began to publish her original Hebrew poems, Hebrew in the United States already held the status of a foreign language, while in Israel it was already a dominant national vernacular. It is in this context that Farmelant published the poem *"Iyov"* ("Job") in Israel in 1948, just a few months after the establishment of the State of Israel.[7]

Translating Farmelant required that I acknowledge that this language came "naturally" for the poet and that I reflect on my own biases, as someone who acquired her Hebrew in an Israeli context. In my translations, I wanted to acknowledge the poet's ease with Hebrew, while also avoiding the temptation to smooth over peculiarities of syntax and idiom. At any rate doing so can have disastrous outcomes for the translation of poetry, which on principle pushes language out of its comfort zones. Over time I felt increasingly at home in Farmelant's Hebrew, in large measure because of the close reading that translating a poem requires. Alan Mintz's description of the process of reading and contextualizing the texts that formed his study of American Hebrew poetry resonated with my own:

> In the absence of translations and any real critical literature, both signs of the long neglect of the subject, I found it challenging simply to read through the material and block out a general mapping of the poet's oeuvre. It was akin, to press the metaphor, to cutting a path through a virgin forest. At first acquaintance, if truth be told, I often found the poet's verse daunting and uninviting. With persistence, however, the veil of difficulty would lift and the poetry would become differentiated and approachable. Afforded free movement within the poetry, finally, I could locate the individual poems that spoke to me and immerse myself in them. And thus, in stages and over time and somewhat unexpectedly, I would, almost without exception, fall in love with the poet I was working on at the time.[8]

Portrait of Annabelle (Chana) Farmelant, Bachrach Studios, date unknown. Courtesy of Annabelle (Chana) Farmelant.

The "free movement" Mintz describes also shaped my final selection of poems. I discern now, as I read the final manuscript, a consistent preoccupation with themes, figures, and language of movement, travel, and migration. It isn't incidental that I chose to translate many poems that are *'al pi,* or "after," other poems: among them, "The Unwed Maiden," after Sappho's Fragment 105a;

"Farewell, Love," after Byron's "So, we'll go no more a roving"; and "Jealousy," after Dylan Thomas's "On the Marriage of a Virgin." Farmelant's intertextuality leans heavily, as one would expect, on biblical material, as well as on her engagement with Hebrew poets like Hayim Nahman Bialik and Eisig Silberschlag; but intertextual threads that connect her work beyond the Hebrew and Jewish frames are evident in Farmelant's own work of translation and adaptation. If I gravitated to these poems, it is because they acknowledge, as does "The World Is Like a Poem," that original works are unmoored, restless, and nomadic.

In a brief review of *Iyyim bodedim,* published in *Moznayim* in 1960, the critic and editor Moshe Ben-Shaul made the following observation: "[These poems] carry something of the style of fin-de-siècle English poetry in their distinct Modernist flavor, especially with regard to the image and the musicality of contemporary language and . . . definitely modern concepts."[9] In my conversations with Farmelant, she consistently resisted any attempt to identify her influences or to affiliate her with the prevailing groups and movements of early to mid-twentieth-century Hebrew poetry. Nevertheless, Farmelant's emphasis on the fragment and image aligns her work with the modernism of H.D. in English and Esther Raab in Hebrew. For the most part Farmelant's poetry does not adhere to classical forms and prosody, and her intertextuality—compared to the more densely allusive poetry of early twentieth-century American Hebrew—is relatively transparent. Notwithstanding Farmelant's resistance to the pull of influence on her work, the words *'al pi* suggest a wide network that my translations recast and reengaged with the hope that new readers will send the poems off on new wanderings—"always, always."

Selections from *Desert Islands*[1]

איים בודדים

בְּאִיֵּי חַיִּים מָוֶת וְאַהֲבָה
כֻּלָּנוּ מַפְלִיגִים
בְּלִי מָשׁוֹט וּבְלִי קַבַּרְנִיט
אָנוּ שָׁטִים עִוְרִים.
יְעוּדֵנוּ לָרוּחַ מֻפְקָד,
לִנְסִיעָתֵנוּ אֵין כַּוָּנָה
בֵּין אִי לְאִי, בֵּין יָם לְיָם
הַגֶּשֶׁר הוּא הַזְּמָן.

Desert Islands

On islands of life, death, and love
we are all sailors
without an oar or captain
blind oarsmen.
Our destination is in the wind's hands,
our journey has no purpose.
Between islands and seas
the bridge is time.

רגע

בֵּין מֶרְחָק וּזְמַן
רֶגַע קַיָּם
רֶגַע נֶעֱלָם.
קְטַנְתִּי מִלִּקְרֹא "דָּם"
כְּבֶן־נוּן
"בְּגִבְעוֹן וּבְאַיָּלוֹן"
הָרִאשׁוֹן וְהַשֵּׁנִי
וְכֹה כֻּלָּם
אֲדָמָה עֲדֵי
יִכְווּ בְּשִׁירַי.

Moment

Between space and time
a moment comes
a moment goes.
I am unworthy to cry out "Be still!"
like the son of Nun
"in Gibeon and Ayalon."[2]
One and the other
then everyone
I will compare until
they are sealed in my poem.

"העלמה שלא התחתנה"

על פי שיר של סאפפו

"עַל זַלְזַל עֶלְיוֹן
מִתְאַדֵּם תַּפּוּחַ."
שָׁם קַן הָעַלְמָה
בַּשָּׁלָב הַתַּחְתּוֹן:
מְזַמְזְמוֹת הַנָּשִׁים
כַּדְּבוֹרִים בְּחוּגֵי הַגְּבָרִים.
עַלְמָה אַחֲרֵי הַבָּצִיר, הַמָּסִיק,
בֵּין רִבּוֹא קוֹטְפִים
לֹא יָכְלוּ הַשִּׂיגֵךְ?

"The Unwed Maiden"

after a poem by Sappho[3]

"On the twig above[4]
an apple reddens."
The maiden's nest rests
on the lower step;
The women buzz
like bees in the company of men.
Still virgin after the vintage and oil harvest—
Among these thousands of gatherers
not one was able to pluck you?

שיר בסתיו

כְּעוּסִים הַשָּׁמַיִם מִתְכַּוְּצִים
הָרוּחַ הַגֵּא כַּנֶּשֶׁר מְרַחֵף
וּפְחָדִים עַתִּיקִים בַּלֵּב מִתְחַבָּאִים.
כֻּלָּנוּ נוֹטִים לָמוּת!
הִתְפָּרֵץ בִּתְאַוָּה הָעֵץ
בְּחַיִּים, טֶרֶם גּוֹסֵס
וְצֶבַע בְּרַבְגּוֹנִיּוּת
אֶת יְהָבֵנוּ עַד אֵין קֵץ.

A Song of Autumn

Enraged the sky shrinks.
The lofty wind hovers like an eagle
and ancient fears lurk in the heart.
We are all dying!
The tree burst with longing—
with life—before it fell
endlessly painting
our lot[5] in many colors.

POEMS BY ANNABELLE (CHANA) FARMELANT

מתחדש הסהר

"אֵין חָדָשׁ תַּחַת הַשֶּׁמֶשׁ"
מַה מְּשַׁעֲמֵם לָנוּ קֹהֶלֶת.
אוּלַי הַסַּהַר יָקִם אֶת נִקְמָתוֹ
מֵחֲמִימוּת הַשֶּׁמֶשׁ הָעַתִּיקָה.
יוֹם יִהְיֶה לַיְל וְנַהְפֹּךְ בּוֹ.
נַעֲמֹד עַל רֹאשֵׁנוּ
וְרַגְלֵנוּ, אֶרֶשׁ שְׂפָתֵנוּ
סִלְחִי לָנוּ שֶׁמֶשׁ רְחוֹקָה
אֵיךְ נִגַּע בָּךְ?
אַתְּ תָּמִיד בּוֹעֶרֶת.
הַסַּהַר דּוֹדֵנוּ הָרַךְ
הַפַּיְטָן לָטֻף בְּקוּלְמוֹס
אוֹתְךָ הַמַּדְעָן יִתְקֹף
כִּי אֵין סוֹף לַבּוּלְמוּס

קְרוֹבֵי סַהַר אָנוּ.
מַכֵּי סַהַר אָנוּ
קָטְבֵי עוֹלָם עָמְדוּ
דֹּם! וְנַחְדֹּר מֵהָלְאָה?
נִפְשֹׁט אִצְטְלָה אֱנוֹשִׁית
וְנִגְלֹם גְּלִימָה מְכוֹנָאִית
רוֹבּוֹטָא תֵּלֵד רוֹבּוֹטָא.
וְאוּלַי יָשִׂים קֵץ הָאֵל
לְמְכוֹנַת הַהַפְלָגָה
בִּתְקוּפַת הַסַּהַר
לְמַכֵּי הַסַּהַר.
רוֹבּוֹטָא*—

* רוֹבּוֹטָא—.Robot

New Moon

"There is nothing new under the sun."[6]
Kohelet bores us so.
Maybe the moon will strike revenge
on the sun's ancient glow.
Day becomes night and vice versa.
We'll stand on our heads
our feet, our lips will speak:[7]
forgive us, distant sun,
how will we touch you?
You always burn.
Our moon, tender beloved
caressed by the *paytan*'s stylus[8]
yet attacked by the scientist
for hunger is bottomless[9]

We are lunar kin.
Moonstruck.
Earth's axes, stand
still![10] How far will we go?
We'll remove our human vestment
and fashion a mechanical robe.
Robot will beget robot.
But maybe god will put an end
to the sailing machine
of the moon age
for the moonstruck.

POEMS BY ANNABELLE (CHANA) FARMELANT

גּוֹרֵד שְׁחָקִים

יֶלֶד, הַכִּכָּר שָׁטוּחַ
זְהִירוּת, הַמּוֹרָד שָׁקוּעַ
מוּלְךָ, הַשַּׁחַק. עָצוּם.
תְּכַסֵּהוּ, הוּא עֵירֹם
תִּהְיֶה לְאִישׁ, כְּאָדָם הָרִאשׁוֹן
אֶת כָּל הַשְּׁחָקִים תִּגְרֹד
לְאַט יֶלֶד, הַיָּם עָמֹק.
תַּעֲמִיק מֵעַל
הֱיֵה אִישׁ חָלָל.

Skyscraper

Child, the plaza is flat.
Take care, the slope sets
before you, the sky, immense.
It's naked. Cover it.
You will be a man, like Adam
you will scrape the whole sky.
Slowly, child, the sea is deep.
Descend up.
Spaceman.

סַגִּי נְהוֹר

וַיְהִי בַדֶּרֶךְ לִירוּשָׁלַיִם
תַּחֲנָה לְלֹא בֵינַיִם,
יָצָא סַגִּי נְהוֹר
שֶׁאֶצְלוֹ מְשַׁמְּשִׁים אוֹתוֹ גֹּדֶל
הַשֶּׁמֶשׁ וְהַסַּהַר.
פִּתְאֹם נִזְכַּר בְּמִלְחֶמֶת
בְּנֵי חֹשֶׁךְ וּבְנֵי אוֹר
וְזָעַק: אֵי הַיְצִיאָה
הַדֶּרֶךְ לִדְרוֹר?
עֵינָיו: כֶּלֶב וָאִישׁ
מַנְהִיגֵי הָאוֹר.

Blinding Light[11]

On the way to Jerusalem
at a station not halfway there,
exited a blind man
whose eyes equally size
the sun and the moon.
Right then he remembered the war
of the sons of darkness and light
and cried out: Where's the exit,
the way out?
In his eyes: dog and man
guide the light.

בְּמוֹת אֵירוֹפָּה

לזכר משפחת אמי (רוזנבוים) שנהרגה
באירופה בימי הנאצים.

חִישׁ קָרֵעַ כְּמַטְלִית מַסְוֶה
תַּרְבּוּת אֵירוֹפָּה מַתְעָה
הֵבִיא וַגְנֶר תְּחִיָּה לַמּוּסִיקָה
הֵידָד! מוֹחֵא כַף
כָּל יְהוּדִי, עִם כֶּלֶב גֶּרְמָנִי.
הַטּוֹנִים הַקַּלִּים הָרוֹמַנְטִיִּים
וְעִנְבְּלֵי מָוֶת מְצַלְצְלִים.
וַגְנֶר וְחוּגוֹ הַגֶּזַע מְצָרֵף
בְּכוּר רַעַל אֶפְעֶה
הַנּוֹשֵׁךְ דּוֹמֵם וָחַי.
אֵיזוֹ אֶסְתֵּטִיקָה נַעֲלָה
שֶׁסּוּפָהּ לָרֶדֶת מֵעַל הַבָּמָה.
לֹא נִשְׁלֹל גַּם אֶת הַהוֹגִים
אֲשֶׁר בְּהִרְהוּרֵיהֶם הָרִים בּוֹקְעִים.
עַל פִּי הַדִּיאָלֶקְטִיקָה הַיְשָׁנָה
הַמְאַלֶּפֶת אֶת כָּל הַתּוֹרָה
אֶפְשָׁר גַּם שֶׁקֶר לֶאֱמֶת,
אֵיךְ לֹא צוֹדְקִים הָרוֹצְחִים
שֶׁיָּנְקוּ תוֹרָה מִתַּרְבּוּת אֵירוֹפָּה
שֶׁהִיא שִׂיא הַשִּׂיאִים.
בַּעֲקִיפִין וּבְמֵישָׁרִין הָאִידֵיאוֹלוֹגְיוֹת
כִּסּוּ אֶת הַזְּמַן כְּקֶרַח דַּקִּיק
וְהֶחֱזִירוּ אֶת הָאָדָם לִטְרוֹם בְּרֵאשִׁית.
אֵין הֵד וְאֵין תַּצְפִּית לַלַּבָּה הַמִּסְתַּתֶּרֶת
בְּרַגְבֵי נְבָכֶיהָ מִתְפָּרֶצֶת
אֵירוֹפָּה בּוֹעֶרֶת בּוֹעֶרֶת בָּאֵשׁ.
הַתְּזוּזוֹת, וְהָאַנְטִיתְזוֹת שֶׁל הַמַּעֲרָב
וּמַה בָּא אַחַר הַזִּוּוּג הַגָּדוֹל
הַסִּינְתֵּזָה עָלַת הָעִלּוֹת.
בְּגִינָהּ בְּמִזְרָח אֵירוֹפָּה
חוֹלְלוּ מַהְפֵּכָה חֲדָשָׁה בַּדָּם
הַסִּבָּה לְהַנְצִיחַ אֶת הָאָדָם.
לָמָּה אֵפוֹא אֲחוּזִים בְּעוּתִים

When Europe Died

In memory of my mother's family, the Rosenbaums, who were killed in Nazi Europe.

Quick tear this guise like a rag,
European culture is a scam.
Wagner ushered a musical renaissance—
Hurrah! Applause
from every Jew with a German dog.
Light Romantic notes
and death's clappers ring together.
Wagner and his race gather
a fresh venom
with a quiet, fatal strike.
What a sublime aesthetic
descends upon the stage in the end.
We won't even reject the thinkers
cleaving mountains with their reflections.
According to the old
rule-breaking dialectic
even a lie can be validated.
How could the killers go wrong,
when they suckled theory[12] from European culture,
the crème de la crème?
Directly and indirectly, ideologies
covered time like thin ice
and returned man to a precreative state.
No echo or lookout for the hidden lava
bursting from the clods of its depths.
Europe burns and burns.
Theses and antitheses from the West,
and what comes after this great coupling:
the synthesis, the Cause of causes.[13]
Because of this in Eastern Europe
they spun a bloody new revolution
to immortalize man, so they said.
Why, then, did such terror take hold
over a defective idea?

לִקְרַאת אִידִיאָה פְּסוּלָה?
יֵשׁ עוֹד לַעֲקֹר אֶת סוֹד אֱלוֹהַּ
וְיֵהָפֵךְ הָאָדָם לְמְכוֹנָה.
כְּבָר הִתְקַדְּמוּ, הַיָּרֵחַ רַק אָנְסוּ
לְאַט לְאַט אֶת כָּל הַקּוֹסְמוֹס יְשַׁסּוּ.
אַל תִּשְׁאֲלוּ אֶת פִּי אָמֶרִיקָה
לָמָּה הִיא מִתְחָרָה
הָעוֹלָל בְּנַדְנֶדֶת הַזָּהָב
עוֹד לֹא גָּדַל.
אַל תְּבַקְּשׁוּ גַּם אֶת הָאֶקְזִיסְטֶנְצְיָאלִיסְטִים
הַצָּרְפָתִים שֶׁהִקְרִיבוּ עֶצֶם הַבְּרִיאָה
עַל בְּסִיס קִיּוּמָהּ.
הַכֹּל מְפֻעְנָח וּמְנֻתָּח
נִשְׁאַר אֵפוֹא רַק הַמְּגֻחָךְ.
סָב הָיָה לִי, בַּעַל יְעָרִים עֲבֻתִּים
אִינְטֶלֶקְטוּאָלִי, רוֹזֵן הָעֵצִים,
וְלֹא רָאָה כִּי אֵירוֹפָּה מְטֹרֶפֶת.
הָעֵץ נִרְקַב, הַגוֹדָם נָפַל
וְהַזֶּרַע יִדְּפֶנּוּ הָרוּחַ
בְּלִי פִּתְרוֹנִים לְאָמֶרִיקָה
וְצַוָּה לִי שִׁירָה.
חֲבָל סַבָּא. אֵין דֶּמוֹקְרַטְיָה
גַּם בְּחֻקֵּי הַתּוֹרָשָׁה
הַזּוֹרֵעַ אֵינוֹ רוֹאֶה
אֶת פְּרִי הָעֲבוֹדָה.

Uprooting God's secret once again
man will become a machine.
They've already advanced, so far they've raped the moon
but will rend the entire cosmos soon.
Don't ask America
why she's in the game.
The babe in the golden cradle
has to grow up.
Don't ask those French existentialists
who sacrificed creation itself
on the base of its being.
Everything gets deciphered and dissected,
only the absurd remains.[14]
I had a grandfather, an owner of dense forests
an intellectual, a lord of trees,
Europe had gone mad but he didn't see.
The tree rotted, the trunk fell
and in the wind the seed scattered
inexplicably to America
and commanded me to sing.
What a shame, grandfather. There's no democracy
even in the laws of heredity
the one who sows never sees
the fruit of his labor.

טיול אמריקאי—פואמה דרמטית

כל השמות בדויים

נפשות:

הֶרְבֶּרְט לַאי
לִיטִישָׁה (טִישׁ) לַאי אִשְׁתּוֹ:
סְטֶפֶן לַאי (בֶּן י"ג שָׁנָה) יְלָדָיו:
בַּרְבָּרָה לַאי (בַּת י"ז שָׁנָה)
בֶּל בּוֹים: מְבַקֶּרֶת
פְּרוֹפ' מָאנָה: פְּרוֹפ' לְפִילוֹסוֹפְיָה
מַזְכִּירָה
פּוֹעֵל א'
פּוֹעֵל ב'

הַשָּׁעָה 8:00 בַּבֹּקֶר

הרברט: נוּ טִישׁ, דַּעְתֵּךְ עַל פְּרוֹפֶסוֹר שְׁלְתִּיאֵל
בַּטֶּלֶוִיזְיָה אֶמֶשׁ מַה הִיא?
ליטישה: אֵיזוֹ תְּקוּפָה נֶהְדֶּרֶת
אֵין צֹרֶךְ בְּסֵפֶר, בְּדַפְדֶּפֶת;
בִּלְחִיצַת כַּפְתּוֹר
לוֹמְדִים, נֶהֱנִים.
הֶחֱשַׁנוּ אֶת עֵדֶן הָאָבוּד
לָאָדָם הָרִאשׁוֹן וּלְאִשְׁתּוֹ.
סטפן (קָם בְּשָׁאט נֶפֶשׁ): לְבֵית הַסֵּפֶר,
וּמִבֵּית הַסֵּפֶר לַטֶּמְפֶּל
לִלְמֹד אֶת נְאוּם
הַבַּר מִצְוָה שֶׁלִּי.
הַיּוֹם אֲנִי אִישׁ יְהוּדִי.

הרברט: נוּ, יַעֲשׂוּ לְךָ תַּקְלִיט.
הַהַקְלָטָה חוֹשֶׁכֶת בְּעַד הַמַּחֲשָׁבָה.
ברברה (קָמָה): מִי הַמַּמְצִיא עֲבוֹדָה,
הַבֹּקֶר לֹא יָכֹלְתִּי קוּם.
חָזַרְתִּי מִ"דֵּיט"* בְּשָׁלֹשׁ בַּבֹּקֶר
אָז מַצַּב רוּחִי רוּם.

* דֵּיט—פְּגִישָׁה עִם בָּחוּר.

American Trip

A Dramatic Poem
The (Fictional) Cast

Herbert Ley: main protagonist
Leticia ("Tish") Ley: his wife
Steven Ley: his thirteen-year-old son
Barbara Ley: his seventeen-year-old daughter
Belle Boym: Tish's friend
Professor Manne: a philosophy professor
Secretary
Worker A
Worker B

TIME: 8 AM

Herbert: So, Tish, what did you make of Prof. Shaltiel's
TV appearance yesterday?

Leticia: What a marvelous time we live in—
No need to browse books.
With the push of a button:
Learning and Gratification.
We have hastened the Edenic loss
of Adam and his wife.

Steven (gets up, disgusted): I'm off to school
and from there to temple
to study the *dvar Torah*
for my Bar Mitzvah.
I become a Jewish man today.

Herbert: Someone should tape it for you.
Recording has replaced thinking.

Barbara (stands up): Who invented labor?
Today I couldn't get out of bed.
I got back from my date[15] at 3 AM
so I'm in a great mood.

כֻּלָּם הוֹלְכִים. לִיטִישָׁה נִגֶּשֶׁת לַטֶּלֶפוֹן לְבוּשָׁה מִכְנָסַיִם,
מְעַשֶּׁנֶת סִיגַרְיָה.

הָלוֹ, בֶּל; הָלוֹ, טִישׁ.

טִישׁ: נוּ מַה חָדָשׁ, בֶּל? שָׁמַעַתְּ אֵיזוֹ רְכִילוּיוֹת?
מִי מִתְחַתֶּנֶת, מִי מִתְגָּרֶשֶׁת וּמִי יוֹלֶדֶת?

בֶּל: מַחְשָׁבוֹתַי שְׁקוּעוֹת בְּבִקֹּרֶת סִפְרוּתִית.
מַקְבִּילָה אֲנִי אוֹרֶסְטִיס שֶׁל אֶסְכִּילוֹס
לְהַמְלֶט שֶׁל שֶׁקְסְפִּיר.
נִתְקַלְתִּי בְּעוֹד בְּעָיָה:
עִנְיַן כֶּתֶר עֶלְיוֹן; מְשׁוֹרֵר פְּלוֹנִי
סוֹפֵר פְּלוֹנִי לוֹבֵשׁ
וְאֵין שֵׁנִי לְעוֹלָם יוֹרֵשׁ.
רַעְיוֹן הַדֶּמוֹקְרַטְיָה מֻגְבָּל
אֵינוֹ אִינְטֶלֶקְטוּאָלִי בִּכְלָל.

לִיטִישָׁה: בֶּל, אֵחַרְתְּ אֶת הַמּוֹעֵד
לוּ נוֹלַדְתְּ לִפְנֵי מֵאָה שָׁנָה
אוֹרֶסְטִיס, אֶסְכִּילוֹס
אֵינָךְ נָשִׁית. יוֹתֵר מִדַּי גַּבְרִית.
לָמָּה מִן הַצִּבּוּר פָּרַשְׁתְּ
אַתְּ "מְפַסְטְרֶטֶת"*
נִדְמֶה לָךְ שֶׁרוֹדְפִים אוֹתָךְ
בּוֹאִי אִתִּי וְנִשְׁתֶּה קוֹקְטֵיל בַּחֲמֵשׁ
וּבָעֶרֶב נִרְקֹד: "אוּנוֹ דּוֹס, אוּנוֹ דּוֹס"**
טְשָׁה טְשָׁה טְשָׁה***
אוּנוֹ דּוֹס, אוּנוֹ דּוֹס
טְשָׁה טְשָׁה טְשָׁה
כָּךְ אַתְּן פַּרְקִן לְרִגְשׁוֹתַי הַכְּלוּאִים.
אֵינָךְ בֶּל, בִּכְלָל מִן הָעוֹלָם נֶהֱנֵית?
מָה אַחַר הַצָּהֳרַיִם תַּעֲשִׂי?

בֶּל: אֶטַיֵּל בַּגַּן, כִּי אִם בָּא הַסְּתָו
לְצִיּוּץ צִפּוֹר אַקְשִׁיב
בִּמְקוֹם הַפְּצָצָה הָאָטוֹמִית.

* "מְפַסְטְרֶטֶת"—מִלְשׁוֹן Frustrated.
** אוּנוֹ דּוֹס (סְפָרַדִּית)—אַחַת שְׁתַּיִם
*** טְשָׁה טְשָׁה טְשָׁה—שֵׁם רִקּוּד סְפָרַדִּי

Everyone leaves. Leticia reaches for the phone. She's wearing pants and smoking a cigarette.

Hi, Belle. Hi, Tish.

Leticia: So what's new, Belle? Any good gossip?
Who's getting hitched, who's breaking up, who's knocked up?

Belle: I am immersed in literary criticism,
a comparison of Aeschlyus's *Orestes*
and Shakespeare's *Hamlet*.
But I've run into another problem:
The idea of a supreme crown
that certain poets and writers don
but never pass on.
The idea of democracy has limitations
and lacks an intellectual foundation.

Leticia: Belle, if only you had been born
a century ago—
Orestes, Aeschylus—
You're more man than woman.
Why have you rejected the status quo?
Your problem is that you feel
frustrated,[16] persecuted.
Come on, let's grab a cocktail at 5
And then we'll go dancing: Uno, dos, uno, dos!
Cha cha cha!
Uno, dos, uno, dos!
Cha, cha, cha!
I need to relieve my pent-up emotions.
Belle, does the world give you any pleasure?
What are you doing later today?

Belle: I will stroll through the park. As autumn nears
I would rather hear bird songs
than the atomic bomb.
And cast my gaze on variegated
dying trees
that will be reborn in the spring.

וְאֶתְלֶה עֵינַי בְּרַבְגּוֹנִיּוּת
הָעֵצִים הַגּוֹסְסִים
שֶׁבָּאָבִיב חוֹזְרִים.

טיש: בֶּל, אַתְּ לַחֲלוּטִין מְטֹרֶפֶת
מְדַבֶּרֶת כְּמוֹ מְשׁוֹרֶרֶת.
בּוֹאִי אִתִּי, יֵשׁ לִי רֵאָיוֹן
עִם "הָאֲנָלִיסְט"*

בל (עֵינֶיהָ זוֹלְגוֹת דְּמָעוֹת, רַחֲמֶיהָ נִכְמְרוּ עַל לִיטִישָׁה):
שָׁלוֹם, טִישׁ, הַזְּמַן קָצָר, וְהָעֲבוֹדָה מְרֻבָּה.

הֶרְבֶּרְט נִכְנָס לְמִשְׂרָד (בַּעַל תַּעֲשִׂיַּת נַעֲלַיִם)
פּוֹנֶה לְמַזְכִּירָתוֹ: תִּשְׁלְחִי לִי אֶת הַמֻּעֲמָד

נִכְנָס פּוֹעֵל א'.

הרברט: יֵשׁ לְךָ נִסָּיוֹן?
פועל א': הֵן.

הרברט: יֵשׁ לְךָ הַמְלָצוֹת?
מַכִּיר אַתָּה אֲנָשִׁים מְפֻרְסָמִים?

פועל א': אֲנָשִׁים מְפֻרְסָמִים בְּנַעֲלַיִם הֲדוּקִים?

הרברט (פּוֹנֶה שׁוּב לַמַּזְכִּירָה): שִׁלְחִי פּוֹעֵל ב'.

נִכְנָס פּוֹעֵל ב'. הֶרְבֶּרְט מַעֲמִיד פָּנִים
כְּאִלּוּ שָׁקוּעַ בְּמַחֲשָׁבָה.

הרברט: כֵּן, הַכֹּל בְּסֵדֶר, לְאֵיזֶה מוֹסָד דָּתִי
מְסֻנָּף אַתָּה?
לֹא אִכְפַּת לִי קָתוֹלִי, פְּרוֹטֶסְטַנְטִי, יְהוּדִי
וְאִם יְהוּדִי, שַׁמְרָנִי, דָּתִי, רֵפוֹרְמִי
הַפְּתָקִים הָאֵלֶּה, שַׁלְשֶׁלֶת יֻחֲסִין
כַּיָּדוּעַ, עַל כָּל הַפְּשָׁעִים מְכַסִּים.

פועל ב': הַדָּת שֶׁלִּי עִנְיָן פְּרָטִי.
מָה הַמַּשְׂכֹּרֶת, שְׂכִיר יוֹם
אֲנִי, שְׂכִיר שָׁעָה?
לוּ לְפִי רִיקַרְדוֹ שְׁלַּמְתָּ

* אנליסט—פסיכולוג.

Tish: Belle, you're crazy.
You talk like a poet.
Come with me. I have a session
with my shrink.[17]

Belle (weeping with pity for Leticia):
Goodbye, Tish. Time is short and work is long.[18]

Herbert (enters his office—he owns a shoe factory—and addresses his secretary):
Send in the next candidate.

Worker A enters.

Herbert: Do you have any experience?

Worker A: Yes

Herbert: Do you have references?
Know any famous people?

Worker A: Famous people with tight shoes?

Herbert turns back to his secretary.

Herbert: Send in Worker B.

Worker B enters. Herbert feigns concentration.

Herbert: Yeah, sure, no problem . . . what is your religious affiliation?
It doesn't matter if you're Catholic, Protestant, Jewish
and if Jewish—Conservative, Religious, Reform.
These signposts, passed on through generations,
covereth all sins, you know.[19]

Worker B: My religion is a private matter.
What's the salary? I get paid by the day—
What's the hourly rate?
If you followed Ricardo's labor theory of value,
I'd be as rich as you.[20]

Herbert is floored.

The secretary enters apologetically.

(עֵרֶךְ הַתּוֹצֶרֶת) כָּמוֹךְ הִתְעַשַּׁרְתִּי.

הֶרְבֶּרְט נִבְהָל.

מַזְכִּירָה (נִכְנֶסֶת, מְבַקֶּשֶׁת סְלִיחָה): מַר לֵאִי פְּרוֹפֶסּוֹר מָאנֶה לְךָ מְחַכֶּה.

פְּרוֹפ' מָאנֶה נִכְנָס.

הרברט: שָׁלוֹם פְּרוֹפֶסּוֹר מָאנֶה.
אוֹתִי בּוֹחֲרִים לְנָשִׂיא בַּטֶּמְפֶּל
וּכְבוֹדִי, פְּרוֹפֶסּוֹר לִנְאוּם מַזְמִין אֲנִי.
נוּ פְּרוֹפֶסּוֹר, מָה הַנּוֹשֵׂא?

פרופ' מאנה: חֲלוֹמוֹת הַפִילוֹסוֹף
הַמַּדְעָן אָרִיסְטוֹ.

הרברט: סְלִיחָה פְּרוֹפֶסּוֹר, לוּ פְרוֹיד בָּחַרְתָּ
לִנְאוֹם עַל חֲלוֹמוֹת הִרְשֵׁיתִיךָ
מַה לְמַדְעָן עִם חֲלוֹמוֹת?
אִם הוּא מַדְעָן אֵיךְ חוֹלֵם?
תְּנָאַם עַל קוֹדְמוֹ
שֶׁכַחְתִּי אֶת שְׁמוֹ
זֶה שֶׁגֵּרֵשׁ אֶת כָּל הַחוֹלְמִים
(הַמְשׁוֹרְרִים) מִסִפְרוֹ.

פרופ' מאנה: מִתְכַּוֵּן אַתָּה לְאַפְלָטוֹן
אֵינֶנִּי מַסְכִּים עִם גֵּרוּשׁ הַמְשׁוֹרְרִים
מִמְּדִינָתוֹ,
וְאֵינִי לָהוּט אַחֲרֵי הָאִידֵאוֹת שֶׁל אַפְלָטוֹן.

הרברט: אֵיזוֹ אִידֵאוֹת?
נוּ, פְּרוֹפ' מָאנֶה, עֲלֵי לְמַהֵר.
פֹּה מַטְמוֹנִי. פֹּה הוֹנִי
וְכָל הַכֶּסֶף לְמַגְבִּית אֶתֵּן
וִיאַלֵּם אֶת שְׁמִי.

הַשָּׁעָה שֵׁשׁ: הֶרְבֶּרְט חוֹזֵר הַבַּיְתָה.
בַּרְבָּרָה יוֹשֶׁבֶת כְּבָר שְׁעָתַיִם עַל הַטֶּלֵפוֹן
וּמְשׂוֹחַחַת עִם חֲבֶרְתָּהּ.
בַּרְבָּרָה: חֲבֶרְתִּי, אַתְּ שׁוֹאֶלֶת
אוֹתִי אֵיזֶה אֹפִי יֵשׁ לִבְרוּס?

Secretary: Mr. Ley,
Professor Manne is waiting for you.

Professor Manne enters.

Herbert: Hello, Professor Manne
I am about to be elected president of the temple
and it is my honor to invite you to give a lecture.
So, Professor, what will your topic be?

Prof. Manne: The dreams of Aristotle,
philosopher and scientist.

Herbert: Excuse me, if you were to pick Freud
as your topic I would allow it.
But what does a scientist have to do with dreams?
If he's a scientist, how can he be a dreamer?
What about his predecessor—
I forgot his name—
The one who expelled all the dreamers
(the poets, that is) from his book?

Prof. Manne: You're referring to Plato.
I do not endorse the expulsion of poets
from the republic
nor am I a fan of Plato's ideas.

Herbert: Which ideas?
Well, Professor Manne, I'm out of time,
and for me, time is money.
My entire fortune will go to charity
and my name will be immortalized.[21]

Six o'clock. Herbert returns home. Barbara has been on the phone with a friend for two hours.

Barbara: Dear, you ask
what makes Bruce special.
He's a med student.
It's a shame that doctors work so hard—
but they make such a great living!
You know what money and pedigree count for?

רְפוּאָה הוּא לוֹמֵד.
חֲבָל, עוֹבְדִים קָשֶׁה הָרוֹפְאִים
אוּלָם הוֹן מַרְוִיחִים.
אַתְּ יוֹדַעַת מַה זֶּה כֶּסֶף וְתֹאַר?
נְדִירִים בְּאֵלֶּה הַיָּמִים.
הַבְּעָיָה אֵיךְ לְהַשִּׂיג אֶת בְּרוּס.
אֲשַׁנֶּה אֶת קוֹלִי, אֶת לְבוּשִׁי
וְכָבֵס הַקּוֹסֶמֶת יִקְרְאוּ לִי.

בַּרְבָּרָה רוֹאָה אֶת אָבִיהָ, לִיטִישָׁה חוֹזֶרֶת מִשְּׁעַת הַקּוֹקְטֵיל.
הַטֶּלֶפוֹן מְצַלְצֵל שׁוּב. פְּנֵי הֶרְבֶּרְט כְּעוּסִים, נַעֲשׂוּ כְּסִיד,
עַל הַשֻּׁלְחָן דּוֹפֵק, וְצוֹעֵק.

הרברט: אוֹתִי לֹא מִנּוּ לְנָשִׂיא.
פְּרוּטָה לֹא אַתְרוֹם.
וְרַב טְשָׁטְשֶׁל הָרַב
בַּקְּהִלָּה לֹא יְשַׁמֵּשׁ.

לִיטִישָׁה (מִתְפָּרֶצֶת בִּבְכִי):
שָׁכַחְתָּ מָה הַיּוֹם?

הרברט: הַיּוֹם, יוֹם ב'.

לִיטִישָׁה: יוֹם הֻלַּדְתִּי הַיּוֹם.
אֵיפֹה הַמִּינְק* שֶׁהִבְטַחְתָּ לִי?
לְשָׁנֵינָה וּלְלַעֲגָ אֶהְיֶה
בַּ"לָאנְטְשׁן"** שֶׁעוֹרְכִים לִכְבוֹד סִילְבִיָּה
מַה תַּגֵּדְנָה הַנָּשִׁים שֶׁלִּי, הַנָּשִׁים בְּגַת—
הֶרְבֶּרְט לְאִי בְּאִשְׁתּוֹ אֵינוֹ מְאֹהָב.

סְטֶפָן פּוֹתֵחַ אֶת הַהַיְ פַיְ שׁוֹמֵעַ תַּקְלִיט חָדָשׁ, "הִתְנַעְנֵעַ וְהִתְגַּלְגֵּל".
כָּל הָאָרֶץ מִתְרוֹמֵם עַד הַמֹּחַ מִתְבַּלְבֵּל. בַּרְבָּרָה פּוֹתַחַת אֶת הַטֵּלֵוִיזְיָה.
לִיטִישָׁה עֲדַיִן גּוֹעֶרֶת בְּבַעְלָהּ. כָּל הַקּוֹלוֹת הַשָּׁמַיְמָה עוֹלִים!

* מִינְק—מְעִיל (פַּרְוָה)
** לָאנְטְשׁן—אֲרוּחַת צָהֳרַיִם

They're rare commodities these days.
The question is how to catch Bruce.
I'll change my voice, what I wear,
They'll call me Babs the Enchantress.[22]

Barbara sees her father come in. Leticia returns from happy hour. The telephone rings again. Herbert, pale with fury, bangs the desk and yells:

Herbert: I wasn't elected president.
They'll get nothing from me!
And Rav Tschatschel will never run
this congregation.

Leticia bursts into tears.

Leticia: Have you forgotten what day it is?

Herbert: It's Tuesday.

Leticia: Today is my birthday.
Where is the mink you promised me?
I'll be the laughing-stock
of the luncheon for Sylvia.
What will my friends say, those daughters of Philistines—[23]
Herbert Ley doesn't love his wife?

Steven turns on the hi-fi stereo and listens to a new rock 'n' roll record that shakes the whole country senseless. Barbara turns on the television. Leticia continues to scold her husband. These voices rise to the heavens!

שוב לרוחך ציונה

כָּל עַם מַזְרִיעַ זֶרַע לְמִינוֹ
זֶרַע לְחַיִּים זֶרַע לַמָּוֶת
יִשְׂרָאֵל זֶרַע לְאַלְמָוֶת.
כִּי כָאֻמּוֹת תֵּצֵא בַּקְּלִיעִים וּבָלִיסְטְרָאוֹת.
תֵּךְ בַּתֹּף תֵּצֵא יְחֵפָה
בַּגַּ'וּנְגֶל הַבַּרְבָּרִי הַנִּקְרָא אֱנוֹשׁ
שָׁאַב גַּם מֵרוּחַ הֶעָבָר, רוּחַ קַדְמִי.
אִם כִּי כָל רוּחַ בַּר־חֲלוֹף חֲלוֹם נָסוּךְ
רוּחַ יִשְׂרָאֵל, הוּא יִשְׂרָאֵל צוּר מוּצָק
כָּל אֵלֶּה הַמְחַקִּים אֶת הַקְּלִיעִים
הַמְשַׂחֲקִים בָּלִיסְטְרָאוֹת.
הַמְעַבְּדִים תַּרְבֻּיּוֹת זָרוֹת
מַה מֵּעֵבֶר הַגַּ'וּנְגֶל הַבַּרְבָּרִי
הַנִּקְרָא אֱנוֹשׁ?
יִשְׂרָאֵל מָתַאי תֹּאַךְ תִּבְּנִי
אָז תְּבַצֵּר מֶגָלוֹפּוֹלוֹס
בְּרוּחַ יְהוּדִי.

Farmelant's short glossary appears at the end of the original text:
ברברי—Barbaric
ג'ונגל—Jungle
בליסטראות—Ballistic
מגלופולוס—עיר גדולה—Megalopolis

Return to Zion for Your Spirit

Every nation sows its own kind of seed.
A seed of life, a seed of death.
Israel sows the seed of immortality.
Like other nations, she will set off with bullets and missiles.
Striking a drum, she will head out barefoot
into that barbaric jungle we call humanity
drawing also from the spirit of the past, an ancient spirit.
Though every spirit is transitory, a dream cast,
Israel's spirit is hard as flint.
The rest mimic bullets,
play with rockets,
cultivate foreign ways.
What lies beyond this barbaric jungle
we call humanity?
Israel build yourself cell by cell
a megalopolis secured
by a Jewish spirit.[24]

התוכי הישראלי

א

קוֹל הַתֻּכִּי נִשְׁמָע
הִנְנִי "רוֹצָה רוֹצָה
לַוָּן, סִילוֹן, רָקֵטָה
לְלוּכְסוּס, וְסוּפֶּר לוּכְסוּס
הַשְּׁאִיפָה.
אֶת כָּל עַם, גַּם אָמֶרִיקָה אֲחַקֶּה
אֲבָל אֶצְלֵנוּ הַכֹּל יוֹתֵר יָפֶה.
מִתְקַדְּמִים, עַל כָּל מוֹדָה
עֶשְׂרִים שָׁנָה קוֹפְצִים.
מִתְחַרְבְּתִים אָנוּ, בָּרְחוֹב שׁוֹמְעִים
כָּל שָׁעָה שְׁבוּרָה רְצוּצָה
פְּרָט לְעִבְרִית צָחָה.
דָּלִית כַּשָּׁרוֹן, דָּלִית לַהַג
הַכֹּל הוֹלֵךְ אֶצְלֵנוּ
עַל פִּי הַמִּלָּה הַמְסֻלְסֶלֶת
פְּרוֹטֶקְצִיָה."

ב

בֶּחָזִית נָפְלוּ מֵאוֹת בַּחוּרִים
עַל קִדּוּשׁ הָאָרֶץ וְהַשֵּׁם
נִשְׁכְּחוּ לְפִי קֹהֶלֶת
הַכֹּל הֲבֵל הֲבָלִים.
אַחַי הַמֶּרְחַקִּים מַה תַּגִּידוּ
עַל יִשְׂרָאֵל
הַמִּתְפַּלֵּג לְרִבּוֹא מִפְלָגוֹת
קוֹבְרִים אִישׁ אֶת רֵעֵהוּ לַעֲלוֹת,
תְּמוּרַת הָעֲרָכִים רַק דּוֹלָרִים,
לֹא אָשִׁיר לְךָ יוֹתֵר עַמִּי.
קוֹל הַתֻּכִּי נִשְׁמַע בְּאַרְצֵנוּ
וְקוֹל הַזָּמִיר נֶחֱנָק.

The Israeli Parrot

I.

The parrot calls out
"Here I am! I really, really want
satellites, jet planes, rockets
deluxe, super-luxe!
Inspiration.
Every nation, even America, I'll imitate
though things are much nicer here.
Moving ahead, jumping twenty years
over every trend.
We're civilized. On the street we hear
every language crushed and broken down,
except for pure Hebrew.
Useless, speechless.
everything here relies
on that crooked word
Kickback."[25]

II.

On the front line hundreds of young men fell
in the name of God and Country
forgotten according to Ecclesiastes
everything is vanity of vanities.
My cast out brothers, what would you say
about Israel
split into countless parties
burying each other for leverage.
Returns only in dollars.
I will sing for you no more my people.[26]
The voice of the parrot is heard in our land
but the nightingale's song is stifled.[27]

שיר ערש

עֶרֶשׂ הַס, כּוֹכָב רָז
נַחֵם אֶת יַלְדִּי
הִנְנִי רוֹוָה: מָחָר
וְאוּלַי הַשֶּׁמֶשׁ לֹא תִּזְרַח,
כּוֹכָב רָז אוֹרְךָ גַּלֵּה
אֶקְלַע אוֹרֵחַ נוֹשָׁן, הַקְּרָב
מָחָר לְיַלְדִּי הוּא קוֹרֵא.
וְיַחֲנֹק הָאֹכֶל בְּלֹעִי
אִם לְזָרְעַי אֶתֵּן מִפְתִּי הָרָב.
לוּ יָכֹלְתִּי בְּנִי לִמְשֹׁךְ
אֶת הַסַּהַר עַל עֵינֶיךָ כְּמָסָךְ,
יְבַקְּעוּ כָּל פַּחֲדֵי מָחָר
כַּחֲזִיזִים אָז.
אַזְמִין לְךָ שִׁיר כָּרוּב
כִּי שִׁירֵי דַּם אָבוֹת רָטֹב.
חֲזַק וֶאֱמַץ לִקְרַאת
מָחָר הַמְטֹרָף.

Lullaby

Quiet crib, secret star
calm my child.
Here I am, afraid: tomorrow
maybe the sun won't come out.
Secret star reveal your light.
My guest ages before me, the battle[28]
calls for my child tomorrow.
If I feed my progeny this morsel
the food will stick to my throat.
My son, were I able to pull
the moon over your eyes like a curtain
all of tomorrow's fears would burst forth
like sparks.
I'll share with you a cherub's song
for mine is bathed in ancestral blood.
Be strong and bold as you approach[29]
a tomorrow gone mad.

חידוש

נוּם יֶלֶד נוּם
הַסֻּלָּם לֹא מַגִּיעַ הַשָּׁמַיְמָה
פָּרְחוּ כָּל הַמַּלְאָכִים, וְהַתֵּיאוֹרְיָה.
אֵין אֳנִיּוֹת יוֹצְאוֹת לְתַרְשִׁישׁ
מִנַּיִן וּלְאָן עִם הַבַּקְשִׁישׁ?
נוּם יֶלֶד נוּם
פָּרָשׁ עוֹבֵר עַל סוּס לָבָן
סַע מַהֵר עַל גַּב עָנָן.
קוּם יֶלֶד קוּם
תִּשְׁכַּח אֶת הַיָּשָׁן
אוֹתוֹ הַדָּבָר הַלַּיְל וְהַיּוֹם
סַפֵּר אֶת תְּמוּרוֹת הַחֲלוֹם.

Renewal

Sleep, child, sleep
The ladder does not reach the sky
All the angels and theories flew by.[30]
If no ships sail to Tarshish[31]
Where will we take the *baksheesh*?[32]
Sleep, child, sleep.
A rider on a white horse
Swiftly gallops on the back of a cloud.
Rise, child, rise.
Forget old things.[33]
Night and day are the same,
Recount how dreams change.

בלב העולם

בְּלֵב הָעוֹלָם בּוֹעֵר שִׁיר
וְאִישׁ אִישׁ מְחַפֵּשׂ מִסָּבִיבוֹ
אֶת הַנֵּר
חִישׁ חָשׁ הַמְשׁוֹרֵר
בְּמַטֵּה דִּמְיוֹנוֹ
הִתְפַּכַּח הִשְׁתַּכֵּר
כִּי בְּלֵב הָעוֹלָם בּוֹעֵר שִׁיר.

In the World's Heart

A poem burns in the world's heart
and one after another gropes about
for the candle
The poet quickly feels around
with the staff of imagination
sobered and intoxicated
for a poem burns in the heart of the world.

כַּשִּׁיר הָעוֹלָם

כַּשִּׁיר הוּא הָעוֹלָם
בִּכְלִיל הֲדָרוֹ
אַף מֵעֲבִי כְּאֵבָיו,
בְּעוּתָיו וּזְעָקָיו
נִשְׁקָף יָפְעוֹ הַמַּקְסִים.
כְּהֵלֶךְ נִכְנָס הָאָדָם לָעוֹלָם
וְאוֹמֵר לְשׁוֹטֵט בּוֹ
לָנֶצַח, לָנֶצַח.
אֵיכָכָה—יִשָּׁאֵל—אֵיכָכָה
יִמְשֹׁל יְפִי בַּשִּׁיר
אִם שׁוּרָה בּוֹ תִּמָּחֵק?
אֵיךְ תִּקָּרֵן תִּפְאֶרֶת בָּעוֹלָם
אִם צוּרָתוֹ בּוֹ תִּמָּחֵק?
וְלֹא בֶן הָאָדָם
כִּי לֹא בְּשׁוּרָה יְפִי הַשִּׁיר
וְהוּא הֵלֶךְ לֹא־קָרוּא
בְּתִפְאֶרֶת הָעוֹלָם.

The World Is Like a Poem

The world is like a poem
in all its glory,
even in the thick of its aches
terrors and cries
its grandeur is reflected.
Man enters the world like a wanderer
and declares that he will roam
always, always.
But how—he asks—just how
does beauty rule a poem
when a line is erased?
How does splendor shine
when its form is erased?
Man is not in these things
for a poem's beauty is not in a line
an unnamed wanderer
in the world's splendor.

בנאי

שָׂחִיתָ בַּיָּם וְאֵינְךָ
דּוֹמֶה לְדָג
הִמְרֵאתָ עוּף וְאֵינְךָ
דּוֹמֶה לְצִפּוֹר.
בָּנִיתָ מִגְדְּלֵי בָּבֶל
סַתְּרוּ
עָלֵי בֶּן אָדָם הִתְאַכְסֵן
בִּכְנַף הַמְשׁוֹרֵר
כִּי הַנֶּשֶׁר גֵּא וְהַיּוֹנָה רָפָה
וְהוּא מְגַשֵּׁשׁ בְּלִי אִיקוֹפָז
וּבְלִי מִכְחוֹל
בַּאֲפֵלָה אֶת הָאוֹר.

Builder

Though you swam in the sea, you're not
like a fish
though you took off in flight, you're not
like a bird—
The towers of Babel you built
    wrecked
over the man dwelling
in the poet's wings[34]
The eagle is proud, the dove is weak
and he gropes without a chisel[35]
or a brush
for the light in the dark.

לֵית מָאן דְּפָלֵיג

א

הָיֹה הָיָה מְשׁוֹרֵר
עַל עַצְמוֹ הָיָה אוֹמֵר
לֵית מָאן דְּפָלֵיג,
וְכָל הַהוֹגִים, וְאַנְשֵׁי הַמִּפְלָגָה
שֶׁלֹּא הִבְחִינוּ בֵּין חָלָל רֵיק
לְבֵין צְלִיל עָדִין
הִטְבִּיעוּ עָלָיו חוֹתָמָם.
הוּא וְלֹא אַחֵר מְשׁוֹרֵר הָעָם.
מַה נָּתַן לָעָם (חָדָשׁ) שֶׁאֵין לוֹ
יְשַׁעְיָהוּ הַנָּבִיא לֹא לָבַשׁ כֶּתֶר הָעָם.

ב

יִסְלַח לִי הָאֲרִי הַמְשׁוֹרֵר
לְכָבְשָׂה עַל זִכְרוֹ הַמְעֻנָּה לְעַרְעֵר.
אִם כָּל הָעוֹלָם מְכֻוָּץ
הַמַּמָּדִים יָכִילוּ פְּרָחִים חֲדָשִׁים
תֵּן לַנִּצָּנִים לִבְקֹעַ רָאשֵׁיהֶם
וְיָבוֹא הָאָבִיב לְעַמֵּנוּ.

Everyone Agrees

I.

There once was a poet
who would say about himself:
everyone agrees, *leit man defaleg.*[36]
All the thinkers and party officials
who couldn't discern between an empty void
and a delicate sound
still made an impression on him.
He, and he alone, was the national poet.
What could he give this (new) nation that it lacked.
The prophet Isaiah never wore the people's crown.

II.

May the lionized poet forgive[37]
this lamb who dares tarnish his memory.
Were the whole world to shrink
each end would contain new flowers
so let the buds burst forth
and spring will come to our people.

מרחוק לקרוב

הִקְסִימוּנִי שִׁירִים לוֹעֲזִים
וַאֲמָנֵי צִיּוּר נָכְרִים,
אַךְ פָּג הַקֶּסֶם מִלִּבִּי
וְטַעַם הַיַּיִן—מִשְׁפָּתַי.
כִּי יֹפִי נִסְתָּר עָמֹק
מְשַׁכְנִי לִמְקוֹרוֹת אֲבוֹתַי,
לְדַפֵּי מִקְרָא וְאַגָּדָה.
מְשַׁכְנִי כְּלֵב אֵם אֶת בְּנָהּ,
שֶׁהִפְלִיג בַּקֵּשׁ פְּלָאוֹת
בְּאֶרֶץ נָכְרִיָּה.

Far to Near

Foreign poems enchanted me
and painters from strange lands
but this magic passed from my heart
like the taste of wine—from my lips.
For a deeply hidden beauty
draws me to my father's origins,[38]
to the pages of the Bible and Aggadah.[39]
Drawing me like a mother's heart to a son
who has sailed off seeking wonders—[40]
in a strange land.

מחזורים לנשמת אבי משה ז״ל

פְּרִי אֲדָמָה קוֹמֵל, פּוֹרֵחַ
אָבִךָ מֵחִיק הַשַּׁלֶּכֶת הֶחָזֵר
בַּאֲדִישׁוּת סְלָעִים אִלְּמִים.
מֵאַיִן אַתָּה? יֵשׁ מִיֵּשׁ, יֵשׁ מֵאַיִן?
כֹּה מֻפְלָא מְחוֹל מַחֲזוֹרְךָ
בְּלִי שֶׂגֶב וְדִמְיוֹן הַנֶּצַח.
יְלִיד אֱנוֹשׁ, מֵאַיִן אַתָּה
מֵאַיִן עֶצֶב בָּא.

מַה בִּזְבֵּז אָבִךָ
אֻכַּל בְּקִפָּאוֹן וְשִׁדָּפוֹן,
שַׁתֵּף לִבְּךָ לְלֵב הָאֲדָמָה
בַּזְבֵּז אָבִךָ בְּלִי רַחֲמִים מֵחִיקָהּ.
בִּפְנֵי סַרְדְּיוֹט הַזְּמַן הִתְיַצַּבְתָּ
הַנּוֹתֵן לְךָ צַו נִצְחִי,
חִישׁ לְקוֹ הַשַּׁלֶּכֶת.

Cycles for Moshe, My Father Z"L

Earth's fruit withers, flowers
from the mound of fallen leaves your tender shoot returning
indifferent voiceless stones.
Where are you from? Is there a where? a nowhere?
The dance of your cycle amazes
ordinary remembered likeness.
Native man, where you come from
the sorrow comes from.
What wasted your tender shoot?
Worn down by frost and blight
bind your heart with the earth's heart.
Wrest without mercy your tender shoot from its heart.
You reported to Captain Time
and he issued an enduring command:
Hasten to the front line of the falling leaves.

שלום לך אהבה

עַל פִּי שִׁירוֹ שֶׁל Lord Byron
"So we'll go no more a roving / so late into the night"

וּבְכֵן לֹא נִדּוֹד יוֹתֵר
אִם כִּי הַלַּיִל צָנַּה לְאַהֲבָה
דֹּפֶק הָאַהֲבָה לֹא נִמַּשֵּׁשׁ יוֹתֵר
כִּי מְמַהֵר מְמַהֵר יוֹתֵר.
אַהֲבָה נִתֵּן גַּם לָהּ מְנוּחָה
תַּעֲשֶׂה סְבוּבָהּ כַּסַּהַר כְּדַרְכָּהּ.
חֲבִיבָה אַתְּ חוֹלֶפֶת וְיִתָּכֵן
בַּבֹּקֶר אֵינֵךְ חוֹזֶרֶת.

Farewell, Love

"So, we'll go no more a roving / so late into the night"—*Lord Byron, 1788–1824* [41]

And so we'll go no more a roving
though the night be bidden to love.
Love's pulse we'll no longer catch
for it quickens away from our touch.
Love too requires a respite.
She makes her rounds like the moon.
Beloved, as you pass by, it's possible
that in the morning you won't return.

שירה אביבה

מַלֵּי זֶרַע עָקָר
בֵּין הַקּוּלְמוֹס הַנִּשְׁבָּר
לְבֵין הַדְּיוֹ הַיְבֵשָׁה.
בַּת אֵלַד, שִׁירָה אֲבִיבָה;
וְאוֹתָהּ לְעַמִּי אֶתֵּן
לֵאמֹר שִׁירָה.

אִם הִשְׁתַּפַּרְתֶּם מֵאַהֲבָה,
אִם הֶלְאוּכֶם יִסּוּרֶיהָ—
בּוֹאוּ לְגַן הַיַּלְדוּת
וּבְרֵיחוֹת רִאשׁוֹנִים
רֵיחוֹת טְהוֹרִים,
סִימְפּוֹנְיַת־בְּרֵאשִׁית
פְּרָחֶיהָ יָשִׁירוּ לָכֶם.

Shira Aviva[42]

My words are sterile seeds
between the broken quill[43]
and dry ink.
I will bear a daughter, *Shira Aviva*,
and give this spring poem to my people—
and summon poetry.

Whether Love becomes you
or its torments wear you down—
Come to the garden of childhood
and with these original scents,
pure fragrances,
the flowers will serenade you with
a symphony—of creation.

איוב

דַּע לְךָ אִיּוֹב,
כִּי כְּאֵבִים בְּמַעֲמַקֵּי לִבְּךָ
תַּצְפִּין, וְתַרְגִּישׁ מְקוֹר יְפִי
הָאָדָם—כְּאֵב
וְעֵת יוֹסִיפוּ הָעֲצָבִים
לְהַכּוֹת שֹׁרֶשׁ בְּלִבְּךָ
בְּרַח לְךָ אִיּוֹב אֶל
הַשָּׂדֶה, סוֹד הָעֵצִים אֵלֶיךָ,
אֶל חֶמְלָה וְאֶל רַחֲמִים
אַל תִּפֶן כְּדֶרֶךְ אֱוִילִים
בְּשֶׁכְּבָר הַיָּמִים נוֹכַחְתָּ
כִּי חָכְמָה וּבִינָה
גּוֹאֲלֵי אֱנוֹשׁ לֹא הָיוּ.
אַתָּה אֲבִי הַצַּעַר
רִבְבוֹת בָּנִים לְךָ.

Job

Take heed Job,
you will hide deep
heartaches and feel the source
of human beauty—pain
and when sorrows continue
to strike root in your heart
take flight, Job,
to the field, the secret of trees,
pity and mercy,
don't bend[44] as simpletons do,
long ago you were certain
wisdom and understanding
would not redeem humanity.
You are the Father of Troubles,
many sons are born to you.

שינוי, לא שינוי

תַּמָּה הַנְּבוּאָה, לֹא רָצָה הָעֶרֶב רַב
תַּם הַשִּׁיר מַה צָּרִיךְ דּוֹר הַמִּדְבָּר עַכְשָׁו.
וְכִתְּתוּ הָעֵטִים לַחֲרָבוֹת, וְהַגְּנִיָּרוֹת לַחֲנִיתוֹת
צָפוּי בָּעוֹלָם רַק חֶבְלֵי הַחֻרְבָּן
יָד אֶל יָד שְׁכֶם אֶל שְׁכֶם אָחִי הַפַּיְטָן
בָּאֵשׁ וּבְדָם אֶת הַשִּׁיר נַחֲצֹב.

Change, No Change

The prophecy ended; the evening didn't ask for much.
The song ended. What does the desert generation need now?
They pounded pens into swords, paper into spears.[45]
All you can count on in this world is the pain of destruction.
My poet-brother, hand in hand, shoulder to shoulder,
we will chisel the poem with fire and blood.

ארוס

אִם אַתָּה פְּרִי קוּלְמוֹס הוֹמֶרוּס
אִם אַתָּה פְּרִי אֵיקוֹפָז פְּרַכְּסְטִילֶס
אוֹ שֶׁמָּא פְּרִי דִמְיוֹן בִּלְבַד,
אֶרוֹס, אַתָּה גּוּשׁ מֵעֶצֶם וּבָשָׂר
אַהֲבַת נוֹי אָמָּנֵי עוֹלָם
אֲשֶׁר הֻנְצְחָה וְהֻטְבְּעָה
בִּדְמוּתְךָ הַמַּפְלִיאָה הָעַל־טִבְעִית
הַמַּשְׁלִימָה דְּמוּתֵנוּ, דְּמוּתָם הַטִּבְעִית,
הַמִּתְפַּלֵּשׁ מֵחוֹף לְחוֹף מִיָּם לְיָם
מִפָּלֶשְׂטִינָה לְיָוָן.

Eros

Whether the fruit of Homer's stylus
or the fruit of Praxiteles' chisel,[46]
or just the fruit of imagination,
Eros, you are a lump of flesh and bone,
a love of beauty artists have
immortalized and minted
in your striking supernal image
that completes our likeness—their natural likeness—
that drifts from shore to shore from sea to sea
from Palestine to Greece.

Selections from *Flowers of Identity*

שורשים עצובים

גֶּשֶׁם יוֹרֵד
רֶחֶם הָאֲדָמָה
מַפְרֶה.
כָּל דִּכְפִין שׁוֹטֵף,
כּוֹרֵי אֲדָמָה
בֵּין הַשְּׁכָבוֹת
מַשֶּׁהוּ גּוֹרֵד
מַשֶּׁהוּ שׁוֹלֵל מוֹלִיךְ
מִתַּחַת נְהַר דָּם
זוֹרֵם
שֶׁלֶד דּוֹמֵם
וְהַפֶּרַח מֵעָל.

Sad Roots

Rain falls
Earth's womb
    bears fruit,
all who hunger wash away[1]
earth diggers
between the strata
something scrapes
something leads astray
under a river of blood
    flows
a mute skeleton
and the flower above.

תעודת זהות

שיר ילד שהתייתם מהוריו בימי השואה

אֲנִי יֶלֶד רַךְ
פֶּתֶק הִדְבִּיקוּ לִי לַגַּב
הִנְנִי נָע וָנָד
כְּעָלֶה נִדָּח,
הֶעָלֶה נָשַׁר כְּחֹק
מִן הָעֵץ
וַאֲנִי מֵאַבָּא-אִמָּא
כְּשַׂעֲרוּרִיָּה נֶחְטַפְתִּי.
אֶת יַד אָבִי קָשְׁרוּ
לְפָרָה בְּחוּט שָׁנִי
וְהִטְבִּיעוּ עַל שְׁנֵיהֶם
חוֹתָם לֵילִי.
פּוּר לְפָרָה
פּוּר לְאַבָּא
אוֹתָהּ הַכַּפָּרָה.
אֶת גּוּף אִמִּי
הִצְמִידוּ לַחֲזִיר
בְּאַדֶּרֶת בָּשְׁתָּהּ הִתְכַּסֵּיתִי
פּוּר לְפָרָה
פּוּר לְאִמָּא
אוֹתָהּ הַכַּפָּרָה.
אֶת חֶלְבָּהּ הַמָּתוֹק
הִשְׁקוּ דַּדֶּיהָ
צְמוּדָה עוֹד לְפִי
לוּלֵי רַחֲמֶיהָ הָאִמָּהִיִּים
אֶת כָּל בֶּן אָדָם הָרַגְתִּי
בְּתָאֵי תֵּבֵל הַמְסָרְטָנִים.
אֶת אֲחוֹתִי הִלְבִּישׁוּ
בְּשִׂמְלַת מָוֶת לְבָנָה
כִּי נְדָרֶיהָ נָדְרָה לַקְּרִיסְט,
לְפִי צַו הַכֹּמֶר הַנָּזֵר!
שְׁתֵּי נְפָשׁוֹת: אַחַת לַכְּנֵסִיָּה,
אַחַת אוֹת קַיִן תִּשָּׂא.
אֵינֶנִּי יוֹדֵעַ

SELECTIONS FROM *FLOWERS OF IDENTITY*

ID

A poem by a child orphaned in the Holocaust

I am a gentle child
with a sign stuck on my back[2]
I tumble about
like a cast-off leaf[3]
that fell by order
from the tree
like I did from my mother-father
when I was taken away like some disgrace.
They tied my father's hand
to a cow with a scarlet thread[4]
and branded them
with a dark seal.
One lot for the cow
One lot for my father
One atonement.
My mother's body
was bound to a pig
I wrapped myself in her shame.
One lot for the cow
One lot for my mother
One atonement.
Her sweet milk
poured from nipples
still pressed to a mouth
If not for these maternal mercies
I would have killed everyone
in every malignant cell of the world.
My sister dressed
in a white death shroud
to make her vows to Christ,
by order of the foreign priest!
Two souls: one Church-bound,
the other raised the mark of Cain.
I don't know

מִי אֲנִי וּמָה
הִתְיַתַּמְתִּי מִזְּמַן
מָוֶת מֵאָחוֹר
מָוֶת לְפָנִים
וְהָאֶמְצָעִי סָחוֹר סָחוֹר
לְעִתִּים שָׁחוֹר שָׁחוֹר.
בְּבֵית עָלְמִין
זִהוּנִי פְּרָחִים
פְּרָחִים אֲבִיבִיִּים . . .
אֶת רֵיחָם אֶסְחַט
אָפִיחַ בִּנְחִירַי
הָעוֹלָם הַמְעֻפָּשׁ
יִתָּכֵן שֶׁיִּרְוַח לִי בְּמִקְצָת.

who or what I am
I was orphaned long ago
Death ahead
Death behind
The center goes round and around
darkening from time to time.
In the cemetery
The flowers classified me
Spring flowers . . .[5]
I will extract their scent
breathe through the nostrils
of a stale world
that may relieve me a bit.

פרחי זהות

שָׁכַחְתִּי אֶת נִיב הַתְּפִלָּה
כִּי יָצָאתִי בַּבֹּקֶר לָשׂוּחַ בַּשָּׂדֶה
לָשׂוּחַ לְשִׂיחַ שָׂדֶה
וַיַּעְתַּר לִי כַּנָּאֶה.
שְׁכֵנִי שָׁכַח אֶת הַתְּפִלִּין
עָנַד לְרֹאשׁוֹ זֵר פְּרָחִים.
הִשְׁתַּכֵּר מֵרֵיחָם הַיֵּינִי
גַּם חוּשַׁי תָּעוּ כִּי שָׁתִיתִי
מְלֹא הַגָּבִיעַ
וְהִתְפַּלַּלְתִּי מֵהָנֵץ הַחַמָּה
תְּפִלָּה זָרָה
עַד נְעִילָה.

Flowers of Identity

I forgot the prayer's idiom[6]
When I left that morning for a ramble in the field
To ramble with every plant of the field
That inclined my way.[7]
My neighbor left his tefillin behind
And wrapped a garland around his head
Intoxicated by their ripe scent
Even my senses roamed when I drank
The whole cup
And I prayed
A foreign prayer
From dawn to dusk.[8]

הַחוֹמָה

בִּירוּשָׁלַיִם הָעַתִּיקָה מִסְתַּתֶּרֶת
חוֹמָה
וְלֹא נֵדַע אֵיךְ הַהִיסְטוֹרְיָה
כּוֹנָה אֶת הַשָּׁעָה
שְׂרִידִים עַתִּיקִים גִּידִים
וַעֲצָמוֹת יְבֵשִׁים
לֹא יַעֲבִיר אֶת הַזְּמַנִּים.
לְפִי חֻקִּים מוּזָרִים פּוֹעֵם
הַלֵּב לְלֹא פִּתְרוֹנִים.
לוּ הַגּוּיִלִים שֶׁמָּשׁוּ תְּחִיַּת
הַמֵּתִים.
בִּקַּשְׁתִּי אֶת עַמִּי וְלֹא
יָדַעְתִּי מֵאֵיזוֹ בְּאֵר
לִמְשֹׁךְ אֶת עֲתִידִי.
פָּרַצְתִּי אֶת הַחוֹמָה,
מִקְּבָרוֹת אֲפֵלִים יָצָאתִי
לִרְחוֹבוֹת מוּאָרִים
הֵנַפְתִּי מִזְרָח, מַעֲרָב
צָפוֹן וָנֶגֶב אֶת הַקָּרְבָּן
הַמְרֻדֶּמָה.
וְנִדְהַמְתִּי לַחֲלוּטִין
חֶבֶל עָבָה
לֹא יְקַשֵּׁר לִי לָאֲסַפְסוּף
לִי וְלָהֶם אֵין שׁוּם מַשָּׂג
וְכִי עִרְבַּבְתִּי שׁוּב
אֶת הַזְּמַנִּים
וְכִי טָעִיתִי בַּהֲבָנָתִי
אֲבַקֵּשׁ אֶת הָעָם, עַמִּי?
לִדְפֹּק עַל חֵטְא.
אֶת לִבִּי.

SELECTIONS FROM *FLOWERS OF IDENTITY*

The Wall

A wall hides
in Old Jerusalem
but no one knows how History
turned the clock
ancient muscles ligaments
and dry bones[9]
won't budge epochs.
Strange laws dictate
the inexplicable beating of the heart.
Could these parchments revive
the dead.
I asked my people but didn't
know which well
drew my future.
I burst through the wall—
and emerged from grey tombs
into bright streets
I scattered the imaginary
sacrifice
north, south, east, west.
I am astonished in every respect
a thick chord
won't tie me to the masses
we are clueless
were I to mix these
epochs once again
were I to misapprehend
would I ask the people, *my* people?
To strike—sin,
my heart.[10]

הַקִּרְקָס

גִּדַּלְתִּי לִי צִפָּרְנַיִם חֲתוּלִיּוֹת.
בַּגִּלְגּוּל הַשֵּׁנִי אֶתְגַּלְגֵּל
וְאֵהָפֵךְ לְלָבִיא.
אֶתְגַּלְגֵּל אֲחוֹרַנִּית לַקִּרְקָס הָרוֹמִי.
וְיַשְׁלִיכוּ לִי לַזִּירָה
כָּל הַחַיּוֹת עַל שְׁתַּיִם הוֹלְכוֹת
וְאֶנְעַץ צִפָּרְנַי בִּבְשַׂר כָּל
קְטַנֵּי הַמֹּחַ וּקְטַנֵּי הַלֵּב
וְאָקִיא בִּפְנֵיהֶם אֶת עֶלְבּוֹנִי.
הָעֶלְבּוֹן הַסָּתְמִי שֶׁחֶרֶשׁ בָּלַעְתִּי
הַשֶּׁלֶג זֶה כְּבָר נָמַס,
וְהַשְּׁלָגִית גֹּוְעָה
וְלֹא יָכֹלְתִּי לְהַשְׁחִיר עֶלְבּוֹן
הַסָּתְמִי הַצָּחוֹר.
קְטַנֵּי מֹחַ, וּקְטַנֵּי לֵב
לְבָבוֹת רְחָבִים כְּיָם
כֻּוָּצָתָם בִּיוֹן אִוַּלְתְּכֶם
וּמֹחוֹת מַבְרִיקִים
כְּסַנְדָּלְכֹּנִים
הֶחֱלַפְתֶּם בְּאֶבֶן מְזֻיֶּפֶת
שֶׁשִּׁמְּשָׁה אֶבֶן רֹאשָׁה
בָּאִימְפֶּרְיָה.
עַתָּה לֹא תִּצְעֲקוּ "יְחִי הַקֵּיסָר"
כִּי רַחֲמָיו הַמְאֻבָּנִים
מֵעוֹלָם לֹא נִכְמְרוּ
לֹא תִּצְעֲקוּ "יְחִי הַקֵּיסָר"
כִּי כָּל הַקֵּיסָרִים מֵתוּ.
וּבְגִלְגּוּל הַשֵּׁנִי הַגַּלְגַּל
יִסְתּוֹבֵב מַהֵר, וְאֶבֶן
הָרֹאשָׁה תִּסְתַּחְרֵר
יַחַד עִם הָאִימְפֶּרְיָה
תִּהְיֶה לְזָנָב, גְּרָרָה
נִמְשֶׁכֶת
וְהַמּוּקְיָן בִּצְחוֹק יַעֲלֶה
עַל כֵּס הַכָּבוֹד.

The Circus

I have grown myself cat claws.
I'll return in my next life
as a lion.
I will turn back to the Roman circus
and they will send me into the arena.
All beasts walk on two feet
and I will thrust my claws into the flesh
of every dimwit and stoneheart
and spew my shame in their faces.
An ordinary shame that I secretly swallowed.
This snow has melted away
the snowdrop has withered
but I couldn't diminish a shame
so ordinary, so radiant.
You, the stonehearts and dimwits
with hearts wide as the sea,
receded in the mire of your stupidity
minds brilliant
like diamonds[11]
turned into rhinestone
once keystone
of the empire.
Don't shout: "Viva Caesar!"
His hardened pity
will never stir.
Don't shout: "Viva Caesar!"
All the emperors are dead.
In the next revolution the wheel
will roll faster and the key
stone will spin
with the empire
you'll be a tail, a chariot
dragging along
while the jester in stitches rises
onto the throne.

נקמה בטבע

לֹא אוּכַל
לְהִתְכַּרְבֵּל כְּצֵל קִיקָיוֹנִי
הַשֶּׁמֶשׁ תּוּכַל.
לֹא אוּכַל
לְשַׁלֵּב אֶת הַיָּרֵחַ הַשָּׁקֵט
לַשֶּׁמֶשׁ הַלּוֹהֵט.
לֹא אוּכַל
לַעֲצֹר סוּפוֹת
בִּדְמָעוֹת חֲרֵשׁוֹת
וְזַלְעָפוֹת בִּצְעָקוֹת.
יָצָאתִי וְקָטַפְתִּי
אֶת כָּל הַפְּרָחִים
בַּשָּׂדוֹת.

Revenge in Nature

    I can't
wrap myself in the gourd's shade[12]
though the sun can.
    I can't
merge the quiet moon
with the blazing sun.
    I can't
detain storms
with speechless tears
burning heat with screams.
I went out and plucked
all the flowers
    in the field.

POEMS BY ANNABELLE (CHANA) FARMELANT

יַעֲקֹב וְאוֹטוֹקְלַס

לֹא סִפֵּר לָמָּה
אוֹטוֹקְלַס מְסִיסִיפִיּוּס
בְּהֵמוֹת גָּנַב
וְהֶחְלִיף צִבְעָם.
לֹא סִפֵּר אֵיךְ מְקוֹרִינְט
לִכְנַעַן לְיַעֲקֹב
אֶת הַסּוֹד הֵחִישׁ.
הָאֵמוֹת מְסַפְּרִים
כִּי סִיסִיפִיּוּס גִּבּוֹר.
הָאֵמוֹת מְסַפְּרִים
כִּי לָבָן צָחוֹר
לְפִי הָעַיִן וְהָעוֹר
וְיַעֲקֹב יוֹדֵעַ לְהַחְלִיף
צְבָעִים.

Jacob and Autolycus[13]

It's never clear why
Autolycus swiped
Sisyphus' herd
and changed its color.
How he hastened this secret
from Corinth to Canaan
into the hands of Jacob.
Nations claim
Sisyphus is a hero.
Nations claim
white is white
by touch and by sight
but Jacob knows how to change
colors.

הקנאה

על פי שירו של
Dylan Thomas
"On the Marriage a Virgin"

הַשֶּׁמֶשׁ בָּא כְּגַנָּב
הַפַּעַם כְּזָכָר
מִבַּעַד הָאֶשְׁנָב.
רָאָה הַבְּתוּלָה
בִּזְרוֹעוֹת הַדּוֹד
וַתִּךְ עַל רֹאשׁוֹ.
בְּאֵשׁוֹ הַגָּדוֹל
לֹא יָכוֹל
בְּתוּלֶיהָ, לִבְעֹל,
בְּקִנְאָה אִשִּׁית
קָפַץ עַל יְרֵכָהּ
וּצְרָבָהּ.

Jealousy

after Dylan Thomas's poem "On the Marriage of a Virgin"[14]

The sun broke in
this time like a man
through the window frame.
He saw the virgin
in her beloved's arms
and struck his head.
Even his ardor
won't allow him
her virginity, to steal away,
with jealous pride
he leapt
    and branded her thigh.

נרקיס

זָרִיתִי אַהֲבָה
וְשָׁלַחְתִּי עַל הַיַּמִּים
וְלֹא חָזְרָה הָאַהֲבָה
הַמַּיִם הָיוּ רְדוּדִים.
בְּכָל אֲתָר חִפַּשְׂתִּי
חִנָּם.

בִּבְבוּאָתִי רָאִיתִי
אַהֲבַת עוֹלָם,
בָּבוּאָתִי מֻבְטַחַת
בְּכוֹס שְׁמוּרִים
רֵיחַ הַנַּרְקִיס
לְדוֹר דּוֹרִים.

Narcissus

I scattered love
over the waters
but love did not return
from the shallows.
I searched everywhere
    without reason.

In my reflection I saw
the world's love.
My reflection settled
in a cup of vigil[15]
the scent of narcissus
everlasting.

POEMS BY ANNABELLE (CHANA) FARMELANT

וידוי

קִבַּלְתִּי מִכְתָּב צָרוּב אַהֲבָה
כְּבִיכוֹל מֵאֶרֶץ חַמָּה
כִּסִּיתִיו בְּשֶׁלֶג וְחִפַּשְׂתִּי
קָרְחוֹן עַתִּיק
וְהַמִּלִּים אֲהַבְתִּיךָ בַּסֵּתֶר
הַנַּעֲלָה בַּפָּנוֹת
כְּחִצִּים שְׁלוּחִים שֶׁהֶחֱטִיאוּ
אֶת הַמַּטָּרָה
וְחוֹזְרִים כְּשַׁעֲוָה כְּעוּרָה
כְּמוֹ נֵר שֶׁדָּלַק וְכָבָה.

Confession

Singed with love the letter in my hand
seemed to come from a warm land
I covered it in snow and went to look for
an ancient iceberg
the words *I secretly loved you*
above all other women
were like darting arrows missing
their mark
returning like the hideous wax
of a candle that flickered on and off.

בלי פתרונים

על פי השיר

Jacques Prevert, L'orgue de Barbarie
"Tout le monde parlait. Parlait. Parlait"

כָּל הַמְנַגְּנִים מָשְׁכוּ מֵיתָרָם
וְנָשְׁפוּ עַד אֶפֶס נְשִׁימָה
וְאֵינָם שׁוֹמְעִים כִּי בַּבַּיִת
מְמַלְמְלִים מְמַלְמְלִים.
אֵינָם שׁוֹמְעִים כִּי בַחוּץ
הַגַּ'אז מַרְקִיד אֶת הֶהָרִים.
צִפּוֹר מְאַמֶּצֶת אֶת קוֹלָהּ
תּוֹךְ חָלָל רֵיק.
וְרַק הַמֵּתִים בַּיּוֹם וּבְלֵיל
מַקְשִׁיבִים.
אַךְ קָם לִתְחִיָּה קוֹל הָרוֹכֵל
בַּשּׁוּק הַגָּדוֹל, הַמְשֻׁוָּק
אֶת הַמֶּלֶל הַזּוֹל.

SELECTIONS FROM *FLOWERS OF IDENTITY*

A Riddle

"Tout le monde parlait / parlait parlait"—Jacques Prévert, "L'Orgue de Barbarie"[16]

The players strained their strings
and blew until they turned blue
and now don't hear anything, at home
everyone talks talks talks.
They hear nothing, outside
jazz makes the mountains dance.
A bird's voice swells
into an empty space.
Only the dead listen
day and night.
But the peddler's voice comes to life
in the big market that hawks
cheap talk.

נשיקת הדבורה

מִמָּה נִפְטַר מַר אִיקְס
הַתּוֹכְסוֹלוֹגִים לֹא קָבְעוּ
הֲשֶׁלָּךְ הַס: כֻּלָּם מֵתוּ.

כִּבְשָׂה שׁוֹכֶבֶת עִם אַרְיֵה
כֶּלֶב עִם חָתוּל
בְּאַחֲרִית הַיָּמִים
זֶה הֶחָזוֹן שֶׁחָזוּ.

הָאִיזְמִים הַפּוֹלִיטִיִּים בְּמָחוֹל
יָצְאוּ
הָאִיזְמִים הַפּוֹלִיטִיִּים אִישׁ
בְּאָחִיו הִתְנַקְּשׁוּ
אֵין אֲוִיר, אֵין נְשִׁימָה
קוֹל הַדְּבוֹרָה נִשְׁמַע.
מַר אִיקְס אָכַל דְּבַשָּׁה
עַכֵּל נְשָׁרַת אַרְסָהּ.

כְּזוּבָהּ דְּבַשַׁת הָאִיזְמִים
נְשִׁיקַת הַדְּבוֹרָה בָּהּ
אֲטוּמָה
בִּזְנוּנִים, כָּל מְאַהֲבֶיהָ
מְפַתָּה.

The Bee's Kiss

What killed Mr. X
the toxicologists could not say
Silence: Everyone died.

A lamb lies with a lion
a dog with a cat
in the final days
they envisioned this.

The political isms broke
into a jig
the political isms put out
a fratricidal hit.[17]
Airless, breathless
the bee's voice is audible.
Mr. X ate her clover,
digesting the dregs of her poison.

In the deceptive nectar of isms
the bee's kiss
is sealed
all of her lovers wantonly
tempted.

שתי מזוזות

שְׁתֵּי מְזוּזוֹת מָשׁוּ, מִן הַיָּם
אַחַת דְּלִי מַיִם, שְׁנִיָּה פְּנִינִים
הָעָם אֶת הַפְּנִינִים דָּחָה, וְהַמַּיִם שָׁתָה.
כִּי בַּצֹּרֶת בָּאָרֶץ כָּל הַשָּׁנָה,
יָצָא הָעָם שׁוּב לִרְווֹת צְמָאוֹנוֹ.
הָלוֹךְ וְשׁוֹב הַנּאדִי כָּזוּב.
וְאֵי מִשָּׁם בְּאֶרֶץ רְחוֹקָה בִּקְּשׁוּ
כָּל הַכּוֹרִים וְכָל הַדּוֹלִים
אֶת הַמְּזוּזָה הַחוֹרֶזֶת פְּנִינִים.
הִיא הִשִּׁילָה דֶּמַע רַב־גּוֹנִי לְמַזְכֶּרֶת.
לְמַרְגְּלוֹת הֶהָרִים, לְחוֹף הַמּוֹלֶדֶת
וְהָעָם זָכַר, בָּכָה כָּל הַשָּׁנָה.

Two Muses

Two muses drew from the sea
a pail of water and a pail of pearls.
The people rejected the pearls and drank the water.
Drought plagued the land all year,
to quench their thirst they set out again
and again for the illusive stream.
Somewhere in a distant land
the diggers and diviners sought out
the pearl-stringing muse.
She shed a colorful tear as a souvenir.
At the foothills, on the homeland's shore
there the people remembered and wept all year.

POEMS BY ANNABELLE (CHANA) FARMELANT

גשרים

בְּיַלְדוּתִי בָּנִיתִי
אַרְמוֹנוֹת מְלָכִים, מִגְדָּלִים
שֶׁנְהַבִּיִּים,
וּגְשָׁרִים פְּשׁוּטִים.
סָתַרְתִּי אֶת כֻּלָּם
וְשָׁמַרְתִּי עַל הַגְּשָׁרִים הַפְּשׁוּטִים.
וְכִי גוּפִי פָּשַׁט צוּרָה
וְלָבַשׁ צוּרָה
אֵין פַּעַר בֵּין יַלְדוּתִי
הַבַּגְרוּת, וְכָל הַכַּנּוּת
לְבֵינִי.

Bridges

In my childhood I built
royal palaces,
ivory towers
and simple bridges.
I destroyed everything
but the simple bridges.
And so my body shed its form
and reformed—
no gap remains between childhood,
getting older, all that candor
and me.

קווים מטושטשים

מִי אָמַר אַחַר הַגֶּשֶׁם
שֶׁמֶשׁ תֵּצֵא
אַחַר הַגֶּשֶׁם הַשֶּׁמֶשׁ
בְּקַרְנֵי הַשּׁוֹאָה מִתְחַבֵּא
לְשָׁנָיהּ, לְשָׁנִים וְלִנְצָחִים.
מִי אָמַר כִּי תְּכֵלֶת הַיּוֹם
מֵאֵפוֹר הַלַּיְלָה תִּפָּרֵד.
בְּחִלּוּפֵי מַסֵּכוֹת
תְּכֵלֶת וָאֵפֶר
יוֹצְאִים בִּמְחוֹלוֹת
מִי אָמַר כִּי אֲוִיר
מִפְּנֵי עֲרָפֶל דּוֹחֶה
עָנָן בְּכוֹכָב תּוֹעֶה.
אִישׁ בִּצְעָקָה עֲכוּרָה
פָּתַח אֶת דֶּלֶת
הָעוֹלָם וּסְגָרָהּ.

Blurred Lines

Who said the sun comes out
after it rains?
After rain the sun hides
for a second, for years, forever
in the rays of catastrophe.[18]
Who said day's blue
would break from night's gray?
In a masquerade
blue and gray
pair up to dance.
Who said that air
fades before the fog
a cloud lost in a star?
With a grim shout a man
opened the door
of the world and closed it shut.

מרוץ לכוכב

יֵשׁ כּוֹכָבִים גְּדוֹלִים
וְיֵשׁ כּוֹכָבִים קְטַנִּים.
כֻּלָּנוּ אַחֲרֵי אֶחָד
רוֹדְפִים.
כְּחוּגָה מִסָּבִיבוֹ
רוֹקְדִים.
הַרְבֵּה אֲנָשִׁים
וְכוֹכָב אֶחָד
וְאֵין מַזָּל.

Race to the Star

There are big stars
And small stars
We all chase after
One star
We dance around it
Like a dial
A lot of us
One star
No luck

עפיפון

כִּי נִמְתְּחוּ מֵיתְרֵי הָעֲצַבִּים
כִּי מְנַגֵּן הַכַּנָּר
אֶת הַפִּזְמוֹן הַיָּשָׁן
הֲבֵל הֲבָלִים
זְרֹק אֶת כָּל הַחֲבָלִים.

תִּקַּח חוּט דַּק
וַעֲפִיפוֹן בּוֹ תִּקְשֹׁר
וְהָרוּחַ שִׁיר חָדָשׁ יָשִׁיר
עֵת הָעֲפִיפוֹן בִּכְנָפָיו
מַשִּׁיק אֶת הָאֲוִיר.

הַנְּשָׁרִים וְגוֹרְדֵי שְׁחָקִים
קוֹמָתָם מַנְמִיכִים
וְהַיְלָדִים בִּצְחוֹק שָׁמַיִם
מַסִּיקִים.
הָעֲפִיפוֹן עָף וְעָף.

Kite

Because the nerves
    are stretched tight
Because the violinist plays[19]
that old tune
    vanity of vanities
let the strings go.

Take a thin thread
and tie a kite with it.
The wind will sing a new song
when the wings of the kite
graze the air.

The eagles and skyscrapers
    descend
and children laughing
    agitate the sky.
The kite flies and flies.

בשל ציפור

בֵּין מִפְלָשִׁים לַעֲרָפָל
קוֹלֵךְ הַדַּקָּה צְפוֹרִי
עוֹדֶנִּי מַאֲמִינָה בְּקוֹלֵךְ
הַדַּקָּה
הַמַּשְׁתֶּקֶת אֶת קוֹל הַבָּרָק
אֶת הַמּוּעָקָה עַל נַפְשִׁי
עוֹדֶנִּי מַאֲמִינָה בְּקוֹלֵךְ הַדַּקָּה
הַמַּקִּישָׁה עַל מֵיתָרִים דּוֹמְמִים
נוֹצָתֵךְ הַדַּקָּה הַחוֹתֶמֶת
עַל שִׁירַי
שַׁרְתִּי וְשַׁרְתִּי.

For a Bird

Between corridors and fog
your tender voice, my bird,
I still believe in this
tender voice
that arrests a clap of lightning
the weight on my soul
I still believe in this tender voice
that strikes quiet strings
your tender quill that signs
my poem
I was singing and singing.

Notes

Notes to Introduction: "Meager Gifts" from "Desert Islands"

1. Alan Mintz, "Hebrew Literature in America," in *The Cambridge Companion to Jewish American Literature,* ed. Hana Wirth-Nesher and Michael P. Kramer (Cambridge: Cambridge University Press, 2003), 92–109.

2. Stephen Katz, *Red, Black, and Jew: New Frontiers in Hebrew Literature* (Austin: University of Texas Press, 2009); Michael Weingrad, *American Hebrew Literature: Writing Jewish National Identity in the United States* (Syracuse, NY: Syracuse University Press, 2010); Alan Mintz, *Sanctuary in the Wilderness: A Critical Introduction to American Hebrew Poetry* (Stanford, CA: Stanford University Press, 2012).

3. Daniel Persky, "*Parashat sifrutenu ha-hadasha be-amerika,*" in *Sefer Ha-yovel shel Hado'ar* (New York: 1927), 346–52.

4. *Tarbut* ("culture" in Hebrew) was a network of secular Hebrew-language schools in parts of the former Jewish Pale of Settlement, specifically in Poland, Romania, and Lithuania, which flourished in the interwar period.

5. Shlomo Marenoff and Moshe Zalesky, eds., *Ha-'am ve-giborav* (New York: Hebrew Publishing Company, 1950), 155–87.

6. Anne L. Lerner, Anita Norich, and Naomi B. Sokoloff, eds., *Gender and Text in Modern Hebrew and Yiddish Literature* (New York: Jewish Theological Seminary of America, 1992).

7. Ibid, 3.

8. Ibid, 65. This line of inquiry was expanded in Dan Miron, *Imahot meyasdot, achayot chorgot: 'Al shtey hatchalot ba-shirah ha-erets yisra'elit ha-modernit* (Tel Aviv: Hakibutz Hame'uchad, 1991).

9. Kathryn Hellerstein, From "Ikh" to "Zikh": A Journey from "I" to "Self" in Yiddish Poems by Women," in *Gender and Text,* ed. Lerner, Norich, and Sokoloff, 113–44.

10. This corpus of works by (mostly) American-born Hebrew poets begs for a comprehensive study that will describe and analyze the poetry that was produced in this period and published first only in *Niv,* and then also in *Ha-Do'ar,* the main

Hebrew publication in America, which eventually began to feature American-born Hebrew women writers in the 1940s and 1950s.

11. Eisig Silberschlag, "The Thrust of Hebrew Letters in America: A Panoramic View," *Jewish Social Studies* 38, nos. 3/4 (1976): 277–88.

12. Walter Ackerman, "A World Apart: Hebrew Teachers College and Hebrew-Speaking Camps," in *Hebrew in America*, ed. Alan Mintz (Detroit, MI: Wayne State University Press, 1993), 105–28.

13. This rigorous Hebrew and Jewish education was the same for men and women. This fact explains much of the rise of American-born writers' Hebrew literature in the 1930s, but, as I claim later, the ways in which women like Kleiman and Farmelant wrote was different, as was their reception by the American Hebraists.

14. Mintz, *Sanctuary in the Wilderness*, 252.

15. It seems that both Farmelant and Kleiman also turned to the equally dominant Anglophone male tradition. Farmelant, for example, drew on the work of poets like Dylan Thomas and Lord Byron, who were hugely important for her. As Adriana X. Jacobs argues, drawing from the Anglophone tradition counterbalances the Bialikean influence. See Adriana X. Jacobs, "Hebrew on a Desert Island: The Case of Annabelle Farmelant," *Studies in American Jewish Literature* 34, no. 1, special issue, ed. Kathryn Hellerstein and Maeera Shreiber (Spring 2015): 154–74.

16. Miron, *Imahot meyasdot*, 73.

17. Mintz, *Sanctuary in the Wilderness*, 259.

18. H. L. Gordon, "Ha-meshoreret ve-shirata," in *Kisufim*, by Claire Levy (New York: Pardes, 1941), 11–13.

19. Ibid., 12.

20. *Ha-Do'ar* did publish poems and stories by Hebrew women writers from the *Yishuv*, but Levy was the only American. Only a few American women were published in *Ha-Do'ar* even in the 1940s and 1950s.

21. Stephen Katz, "The Ascent of Hebrew and Jewish Literature in America: Review Essay," *Shofar: An Interdisciplinary Journal of Jewish Studies* 31, no. 1 (2012): 135.

22. In the interview Adriana Jacobs and I conducted with her, Farmelant attested that *Ha-Do'ar* was not sympathetic to her poetry, and attributed it to generational conflicts and tastes.

23. In addition to her poetry, Farmelant's contributions to *Niv* also included an essay on the poetry of Dylan Thomas, with her own Hebrew translation of his poem "Do Not Go Gentle into That Good Night" (1951), and a review of Archibald MacLeish's "J.B," a retelling of the story of Job (1958–59).

24. Shlomo Marenoff, "Hakdama," in *Netafim: Shirim*, by Anne S. Kleiman (Chicago: Ha-Midrashah le-limude ha-Yahadut, 1947).

25. Michael Gluzman, *The Politics of Canonicity: Lines of Resistance in Modern Hebrew Poetry* (Stanford, CA: Stanford University Press, 2003), 101; Wendy Zierler, *And*

Rachel Stole the Idols: The Emergence of Modern Hebrew Women's Writing (Detroit, MI: Wayne State University Press, 2004).

26. As Yosefa Raz notes in her translator's preface, Kleiman has also written a number of poems in what might be called "a major key," influenced by and wrestling with the model of Bialik's poetry and the prominent legacy of his "prophetic poetry." This issue requires further research and analysis.
27. The original Hebrew poem was published in the newspaper *Davar* on August 27, 1926. English translation by Robert Friend in *Flowers of Perhaps: Selected Poems of Rachel*, by Rachel (Bluwstein) (London: Menard Press, 1994), 25.
28. Yael Zerubavel, "Rachel and the Female Voice: Labor, Gender, and the Zionist Pioneer Vision," in *History and Literature: New Readings of Jewish Texts in Honor of Arnold J. Band*, ed. William Cutter and David C. Jacobson (Providence, RI: Brown Judaic Studies, 2002), 303–17; Zierler, *And Rachel Stole the Idols*, 127–86.
29. The translation is by Anne Carson in *If Not, Winter: Fragments by Sappho* (New York: Vintage Books/Random House, 2002), 214–15.
30. This fragment was translated by Aharon Kaminka before Farmelant wrote the poem, but she did not draw on it.
31. Jack Winkler, "Gardens of Nymphs: Public and Private in Sappho's Lyrics," *Women's Studies: An Interdisciplinary Journal* 8, nos. 1–2 (1981): 65–91.
32. See Hamutal Bar Yosef, "The Influence of Decadence on Bialik's Concept of Femininity," in *Gender and Text*, ed. Lerner, Norich, and Sokoloff, 145–69.
33. Jacobs, "Hebrew on a Desert Island," 166.

Note to Poems by Anne (Chana) Kleiman: Translator's Preface

1. See the portrait drawn by her teacher Shlomo Marenoff, quoted in Pinsker's introduction.

Notes to *Droplets*

1. The Hebrew manuscript, published in 1947, is dedicated to the poet's mother.
2. "Spring" is a male noun in Hebrew. I have maintained the male pronoun throughout the poem, as Kleiman eroticizes the male "Spring," an interesting counterpart to the male eroticization of the land in Hebrew poetry.
3. The "*tsafririm*," zephyrs, or morning winds, recur in Kleiman's poetry, intimating a connection to H. N. Bialik's language, especially his poem "*Tsafririm*," in which the childlike play of wind and light, as in this poem, has both spiritual-kabbalistic and sensual undertones.
4. Compare to Bialik's children's poem "*Nadnedah*" ("See-saw").
5. This is an allusion to the biblical expression used to describe Saul's modesty or shyness in I Samuel 10:22: "he hath hid himself among the stuff" (KJV).

NOTES TO *DROPLETS*

6. The footsteps of Spring may allude to the "footsteps of the Messiah" (Psalms 89:52 and Mishna Sotah 49b), the low period just preceding redemption. See also "Again, Spring" for more messianic allusion.
7. See Psalms 104:2 and Bereshit Rabbah 3:4, where God is described as wrapping himself in light.
8. See above, note 3.
9. Isaiah 52:7. Here the romantic tone of the spring poems is overlaid with the prophetic-messianic.
10. "[D]elight" and "cry out for joy" gesture to Isaiah 12:6 "Cry out and shout, thou inhabitant of Zion" (KJV).
11. I consistently translated the Hebrew *adam* as "man," though a case could be made for the more egalitarian "human."
12. See Psalms 8:5.
13. Most literally, "in the narrow place." In psalmic laments this geographical marker always reflects personal distress, thus I echo here the JPS translation for Psalms 118:5.
14. See Isaiah 6:5. Isaiah feels undone and unworthy in the presence of God, who calls him to prophecy. Through this biblical intertextuality, the speaker expresses both distress and modesty but also, at the same time, prophetic aspirations.
15. The verbs in this poem are first-person masculine; they reflect Kleiman's attempt to take on the masculine genre of the prophetic lament.
16. A recasting of Jeremiah 15:10.
17. The reflexive verb "to become iron" is Kleiman's own neologism.
18. Many of the words and phrases are unique to the Song of Deborah in Judges 5, especially verses 6 and 7.
19. See Exodus 13:20–21. This biblical trope is common to Zionist discussions of leadership starting with Ahad Ha'am's essays at the turn of the century.
20. Kleiman may be drawing on the majestic language of Numbers 10:45. In the biblical passage, also a prominent part of Jewish liturgy, the "scattering" of enemies by the divine warrior is made possible by the ark of the covenant.
21. The number here denotes a feminine speaker, a sister to the "brother" winds.
22. See Exodus 15:21, the Song of the Sea, where the phrase is sung by Miriam. In this poem, the sea itself is victorious, as opposed to the triumph of God in the biblical text.
23. See Psalms 114:3.
24. This prophetic declaration of war against the cosmos alludes to the last lines of Bialik's famous poem on the Kishinev pogrom, *"Al ha-shechitah"* ("On the Slaughter").
25. Candles are traditionally burned to commemorate the dead. See Farmelant's poem "Confession" (191).

26. Kleiman often refers to "*tmolim*"—yesterdays, or more formally, days of yore.
27. Literally "Eternal Shabbat."
28. My translation here is partially based on an earlier translation made by Kleiman herself, with her daughter Adina, in the 1980s. The title gestures to the psalmist's imploration, "Consider and hear me, O Lord my God" (Psalms 13:3; KJV).
29. The address to God as *Ha-el* is somewhat distant, formal.
30. See Genesis 1:27.
31. The United Nations Conference on International Organization, a historic convention of fifty Allied nations in San Francisco, took place between April 25 and June 26, 1945, during the very last days of World War II. The conference is reimagined as a scene from the prophecies of Isaiah, referring especially to Isaiah 2 and Isaiah 6.
32. "My words to you" is a typical prophetic address.
33. See Isaiah 2:2.
34. See Isaiah 6:4.
35. In this case, *torah* is used as an indefinite noun, meaning wisdom or teaching, rather than the Jewish scripture. See a similar universal use of *torah* in Farmelant's poem "When Europe Died" (125).
36. See Isaiah 2:10. These last lines are also linked to the triumphant messianic vision of the *'Aleynu* prayer.
37. See Genesis 37:30. This masculine use of the verb alludes to Reuben's despair when he discovers his brother Joseph is gone from the pit. The rest of the poem may refer to Joseph's dreams.
38. *Kaddish* can be said only in a quorum of ten.
39. According to tradition, Rabbi Yohanan Ben Zakkai escaped from a soon-to-fall Jerusalem to establish rabbinic Judaism at Yavneh.
40. A skillful weaving together of Genesis 32:29 and Job 26:7, as Jacob's wrestling with the angel is conflated with the divine mastering of the primordial force of chaos.
41. See Exodus 19, where the assembly sanctifies itself to receive the Ten Commandments.
42. Kleiman dedicated a number of the following poems to her teachers at Hebrew College. See Shachar Pinsker's introduction to this volume.
43. The address acknowledges Deuteronomy 27, where the people of Israel are addressed before entering the promised land: "Take heed, and hearken, O Israel; this day thou art become the people of the Lord thy God" (Deuteronomy 27:9 [KJV]).
44. These lines gesture to Bialik's "*Birkat 'am*" ("The Blessing of a Nation"), which became the anthem of the Second and the Third Aliyah. See also Habakkuk 3:6.
45. These rousing cries recall the addresses to Zion in Deutero-Isaiah, and their use in the famous medieval *piyyut* "*Lecha Dodi*" by the kabbalist Rabbi Shlomo Halevi Alkabetz.

NOTES TO *DROPLETS*

46. Jeremiah 31:10. In this consoling prophecy, God remembers Israel, imagined as a wayward, beloved son.
47. See I Kings 18, Elijah's dispute with the prophets of Baal.
48. See Ezekiel 37.
49. See Lamentations 1:1. The parents' grief is compared to Zion's grief upon the destruction of the first Temple.
50. Rabbi Akiva was a great rabbinic scholar and a legendary martyr to the Romans. Like the end of Bialik's "*Be-ir ha-haregah*" ("In the City of Slaughter"), which derides the townspeople of Kishinev for being cowards when the blood of the Maccabees streams in their veins, this poem seems to entreat the Hebraists to act in the great, brave, and scholarly traditions of their forefathers.
51. Literally, "Holiness": the most sacred section of the *Amidah* prayer, which quotes the words of Isaiah's and Ezekiel's epiphanies.
52. The biblical expression is "*Hekhal Adonai*" ("The Hall of Yahweh/the Lord"), while here Kleiman uses "*Hekhal Elohim*," perhaps to refrain from the tetragrammaton.
53. Literally, the steering wheel.
54. Abraham H. Friedland was a Cleveland-based Hebrew essayist, poet, and noted Jewish educator, who died at age forty-seven in 1939.
55. A reference to the famous Hebrew symbolist novella by Mordechai Ze'ev Feierberg, *Le'an* (*Whither*), published in the periodical *Ha-Shiloach* in 1899.
56. A pun on Maimonides' *Guide for the Perplexed*.
57. As in the set of poems on Spring, these "zephyrs" allude to Bialik's poem "*Tsafririm*," in which the kabbalistic language of light is used to express pure pleasure and joy.
58. In Jewish-kabbalistic tradition, humans receive a second or "supplemental" soul on the Sabbath.
59. Dr. Nissan Touroff was an educator, essayist, and translator whose career spanned from Russia, to Mandatory Palestine, to Boston, where he founded the Hebrew Teacher's College, and to New York, where he served as professor and dean of the Jewish Institute of Religion.
60. See Psalms 1 for a similar opening formula.
61. The poem alludes to Bialik's long poem "On the Threshold of the Study-House." While Bialik's poem expresses a harrowing ambivalence toward the study house and its walls (both personified as male), Kleiman takes advantage of the feminine gender of the Midrasha, the College of Jewish Studies in Chicago, and imagines it as a kind, maternal presence.
62. Literally, "the intertwining of the ancestors" can also mean "the tractate of the fathers," alluding to mishnaic *Ethics of the Fathers* or *Pirkei Avot*.
63. See Genesis 2:7.
64. An allusion to a line from Naftali Herz Imber's poem "Hatikvah," which was to become the Israeli national anthem: "the eye looks to Zion."

65. Shlomo Marenoff, an educator and essayist, was Kleiman's teacher and lifelong friend. See Pinsker's introduction in this volume.
66. The phrase appears in 1 Samuel 25:6. It seems to have been popularized as a greeting in the 1930s. The 1917 JPS translates it as "All hail!" but I have substituted a more colloquial English expression.
67. See note 44. See also "From the Mountaintops" (43).
68. The speaker addresses "you" as a plural male group. This poem engages the self-effacing "meager poetics" of the 1920s women poets in Palestine, especially Rachel's *"El artsi"* ("To My Country"). See the introduction for further background to this literature and its relation to the work of Kleiman and Farmelant ("The World Is Like a Poem," 149).
69. This statement is somewhat ironic, as the speaker's disavowal of learning and erudition is itself a biblical allusion. See Psalms 142:7, "attend unto my cry / for I am brought very low" (KJV). Cry, *rinah,* can also mean "song."
70. As in the poems "Behold" (35) and "I Only Heard Your Voice" (47), the ancient dual form for seven, *shiv'atayim* (translated as "sevenfold"), imparts a biblical, even prophetic, resonance.
71. The poem is a skillful reworking of the ninth sonnet of Leah Goldberg's cycle of sonnets, *"Ahavata shel Tereza Di Mon"* ("The Love of Teresa De Meun"). In Goldberg's poem, the speaker, a sixteenth-century French noblewoman, addresses her children's Italian (male) tutor, with whom she has fallen in love, by evoking the view shared from their windows. In Kleiman's poem, the speaker addresses a female "sister." In contrast to Goldberg's references to the classical world, Kleiman's poem is rich with religious imagery.
72. These words for light suggest kabbalistic resonances that resemble Bialik's usage. See the first three poems on spring.
73. This language hints at the famous sixteenth-century *piyyut "Lecha Dodi,"* written by Rabbi Shlomo Halevi Alkabetz, which in turns relies on the language of redemption in Isaiah. The poem strikingly turns the allegorical figure of the female *shekhinah* into an actual woman. See also "From the Mountaintops."
74. Possibly a corrective to the story of Jacob and Esau. In this version "sisters" share a blessing rather than fighting over it.
75. See note 22 (212) in "Seas and Wind."
76. Leah covers the speaker with her dress, evoking Bialik's *"Hakhnisini tahat kenafekh"* ("Take Me under Your Wing"), in which the woman is also imagined as the *shekhinah*. See also Farmelant's "Builder" (151), which also alludes to this poem.
77. Kleiman's Michigan evokes Rachel's poems to the Sea of Galilee.
78. Kleiman uses the female noun for moon, *levanah*—literally, "the white one."
79. The image of the huge hand of fate may allude to Rachel's description of a giant malevolent hand in *"Rak 'al 'atsmi lesaper yadati"* ("I Only Knew to Tell about Myself").

80. An allusion to Rachel's poem "*Ve-ulai lo hayu ha-dvarim*" ("Perhaps, These Things Never Were"), from the 1930 collection *Mineged* (*From Afar*).
81. These grammatical forms recall Rachel's famous poem "*Zemer nugeh*" ("Melancholy Song"), in which the speaker asks her lover if her voice will be heard.
82. The verb *nivre'u* (created) has a special resonance with the creation story in Genesis, which I have tried to recreate in the first line.
83. Kleiman's unpublished speech, "The Jewish Woman as a Cultural Force," likely composed sometime after 1960, contains a translation of Anda Pinkerfeld's lines, which probably inspired this poem. In Kleiman's words: "Suffice to point out that [Pinkerfeld's love] is not a love that finds fulfillment; it is a synthesis of pain, suffering, sensuality and longing. It is a self-sacrificing and tender love.

    "I have created you for my longings.
    You are woven through every thread of my life.
    From the heart have I conjured you
    Though you will never be."
    See also Pinsker's translation of Kleiman's essay on Pinkerfeld, p. 95.

84. Literally, "stop and go."
85. Alludes to Shaul Tchernichovsky's dramatic avowal of humanism in the poem "*Ani ma'amin*" ("I Believe"). In the 1947 volume Netafim, the word אתן appears as איתן. Kleiman might have meant something like "while my trust in Man is still strong."
86. See Song of Songs 1:2: "Let him kiss me with the kisses of his mouth: for thy love is better than wine" (KJV).

Notes to "On Anda Pinkerfeld and Her Poetry" by Anne (Chana) Kleiman

1. Anda Pinkerfeld, *Yamim dovevim: Shirim* (Tel Aviv: Zohar, 1929). References to page numbers are from this volume.
2. Anda Pinkerfeld, *Yuval* (Tel Aviv: Davar, 1932); Anda Pinkerfeld, *Gitit* (Tel Aviv: Davar, 1937).
3. Pinkerfeld, *Gitit*, 165–67.
4. Rachel (Bluwstein), "*Yamim dovevim*" (1929), republished in *Rachel: Shirim, michtavim, reshimot* (Tel Aviv: Zmora Bitan, 1985).

Notes to Poems by Annabelle (Chana) Farmelant: Translator's Preface

1. Anne Carson, Interview with Brighde Mullins, Lannan Foundation, March 21, 2001, www.lannan.org/events/anne-carson-with-brighde-mullins, accessed April 24, 2015. This preface includes material that appears in my article, "Hebrew on a Desert Island: The Case of Annabelle Farmelant," *Studies in American Jewish Literature* 34, no. 1, special issue, ed. Kathryn Hellerstein and Maeera Shreiber (Spring 2015): 154–74.

2. See Adrienne Rich's "When We Dead Awaken: Writing as Re-Vision," in *College English* 43, no. 1 (1972): 18–30; Tillie Olsen, *Silences* (New York: Feminist Press at the City University of NY, 2003 [1978]).

3. Michael Weingrad, *American Hebrew Literature: Writing Jewish National Identity in the United States* (Syracuse, NY: Syracuse University Press, 2011), 244.

4. In fact, Farmelant had read the *Commentary* article on which the chapter was based and was compelled to write to Weingrad. "I feel that you should think of me too," she remarked. Annabelle Farmelant, letter to Michael Weingrad, March 31, 2006. See also Michael Weingrad, "The Last of the (Hebrew) Mohicans," *Commentary* (March 2006): 45–50.

5. I compiled this biographical sketch from an interview that Shachar Pinsker and I conducted with Farmelant in July 2010 and from information acquired via various archives and online resources. Adriana X. Jacobs and Shachar Pinsker, interview with Annabelle Farmelant, July 5, 2010, New York, NY.

6. In her extant correspondence with Silberschlag, she did sign her name as Chana Biala Farmelant.

7. Chana Farmelant, "*Iyov*," in *Gilyonot* 21, no. 3 (1948): 114.

8. Alan Mintz, *Sanctuary in the Wilderness: A Critical Introduction to American Hebrew Poetry* (Stanford, CA: Stanford University Press, 2012), xii–xiii.

9. Moshe Ben-Shaul, "Review of *Iyyim bodedim*," in *Moznayim* 11, no. 20 (1960): 142. According to a profile that she submitted to Gnazim, the archives of the Hebrew Writers Association of Israel, reviews of *Iyyim bodedim* also appeared in *Ha-Boker*, *Ha'aretz*, *Herut*, and *Yediot ahronot*.

Notes to Selections from *Desert Islands*

1. Farmelant, like Kleiman, dedicated this collection to her mother, and included in the dedication a quotation (in her Hebrew translation presumably) of W. B. Yeats's poem "For Anne Gregory," which is erroneously referred to in the collection as "To Helen Gregory."

2. "Son of Nun" indicates Joshua, the central character of the biblical Book of Joshua, which includes a famous narration of a battle between the Israelites, led by Joshua, and an Amorite alliance in the ancient Canaanite city of Gibeon. The quotation rephrases Joshua's exhortation, "Sun, stand still over Gibeon; / And Moon, in the Valley of Aijalon" (Joshua 10:12; KJV). By reversing the natural order, Joshua secured additional daylight hours for the battle and increased the Israelites' chances for victory. In Farmelant's poem, the speaker claims not to have this power to suspend narration, but the poetic text, through continuous and persistent acts of composition, becomes the place where this suspension, or sealing, takes place.

3. Farmelant takes her imagery and the opening quotation from an epithalamic poem by the Ancient Greek lyric poet Sappho. Cf. Anne Carson, trans., "Fragment 105a," in *If Not, Winter: Fragments by Sappho* (New York: Vintage Books, 2002), 214–15.

NOTES TO SELECTIONS FROM *DESERT ISLANDS*

4. *Zalzal* (Hebrew, twig) may signpost an allusion to Hayim Nahman Bialik's poem "*Tzanach lo zalzal*" ("A Twig Fell").

5. The Hebrew *yehav*, meaning "destiny" or "hope," figures in the biblically inspired, modern Hebrew expression *hishlikh yehavo 'al*—to pin one's hopes on, to cast one's lot with. "Cast your burden with the Lord / and he will sustain you" (Psalm 55:22; KJV).

6. Ecclesiastes 1:9.

7. "*Areshet sfateinu*" is a traditional Rosh Hashanah *piyyut*, a Jewish liturgical poem. Psalm 21:2, "You have granted him the desire of his heart, have not denied the request of his lips" ("*areshet sfatav*"; JPS).

8. The word *paytan* typically identifies the author of a *piyyut* but can be applied more broadly to mean "a poet," though Farmelant pointedly does not use the modern Hebrew word for poet, *meshorer*.

9. In lines 12 and 14, Farmelant's rhyme—*kulmos* and *bulmos*—brings together two words of Ancient Greek provenance which entered modern Hebrew through the rabbinic tradition. *Kulmos*, a writing instrument, derives from *kalamos*, stylus; *bulmos* characterizes an intense hunger, from the Greek *boulimia*, meaning "ravenous hunger."

10. Joshua 10:12 (see Farmelant's poem "Moment," 113).

11. Farmelant's title "*Sagi nahor*" is Aramaic for "great light" but also refers to someone who is blind. The Hebrew expression "*leshon sagi nahor*" applies to instances of euphemistic and ironic speech, when what is literally stated is the opposite of what is meant. An example of this linguistic play appears in Bereshit Rabbah 30:9, "in the street of the blind, the dim-eyed man is [called] a *sagi nahor*."

12. Farmelant uses the Hebrew word *torah*, in the sense of theory and instruction, but also expects readers to draw connections between the Jewish Torah and the shared biblical patrimony of Jews and Christians in Western Europe. A similar application of the word *torah* appears in Kleiman's poem "To the San Francisco Delegates" (37).

13. The phrase *'Ilat ha-'ilot*, literally, "the cause of causes," is an epithet for God that appears in rabbinical literature, including the *Zohar*, the foundational text of Jewish mysticism.

14. Most likely Farmelant is referring here to the Existentialist notion of the absurd, "born out of this confrontation between the human need and the unreasonable silence of the world." Albert Camus, *The Myth of Sisyphus and Other Essays*, trans. Justin O'Brien (New York: Vintage Books, 1955), 21.

15. In the Hebrew version, Farmelant includes several Hebrew transliterations of English words, which she translates into or defines in Hebrew in her footnotes. The English word *date*, for example, appears in Hebrew transliteration. In the original, Farmelant includes the following note: "Date: a meeting with a young man."

16. The word *frustrated* appears in Hebrew as *mefustretet*. This Hebraized form of the English word appears to be Farmelant's neologism, and to explain its origins, she includes the English word *frustrated* in a footnote. Farmelant also indicates that the "cha, cha, cha" is a "Spanish dance" and that "uno, dos" means "one, two."

17. The word *analyst* appears in Hebrew transliteration, followed by the translation "psychologist" in a footnote.
18. "The day is short, the work is great" (*Pirkei Avot* 2:20).
19. Proverbs 10:12: "Hatred stirreth all strifes but love covereth all sins" (KJV).
20. David Ricardo (1772–1823), an English political economist born to a Sephardic Jewish family, was the author of *On the Principles of Political Economy and Taxation* (1917), which revised Adam Smith's theory of value to include the production value of a commodity. In *The Wealth of Nations* (1776), Adam Smith (1723–90) defined the value of a commodity in terms of its utility and exchange value. Smith, however, did not quantify the value of producing a commodity, or its production value. Ricardo's labor theory of value asserted that the exchange value of a commodity was proportional to the labor required for its production.
21. The Hebrew "*magbit*" (collection, fund) may refer to the United Jewish Appeal as well.
22. In the Hebrew text, this line opens with the sobriquet "*kebs ha-kosemet*," a phrase of unknown origin and possibly a neologism or typo. Farmelant's "*kebs*" could to be related to the root *k.b.s*, from which the words *washing* and *laundry* derive. Given the number of typographical errors in the book, "*kebs*" is most likely an erroneous transliteration of "Babs," a nickname for Barbara. I would like to thank Naama Zahavi-Ely for suggesting this possibility.
23. 2 Samuel 1:20, "Tell it not in Gath, publish it not in the streets of Askelon; lest the daughters of the Philistines rejoice, lest the daughters of the uncircumcised triumph" (KJV). In her notes, Farmelant transliterates "mink" and "luncheon" and translates them respectively as "coat (fur)" and "lunch."
24. The brief glossary that Farmelant appends to this and to other poems is interesting because it raises the question of readership. Words like *barbari* and *balistraot* appear in talmudic sources and are not, as Farmelant's notes suggest, Hebrew transliterations of natively English words, unless, of course, her intent is to emphasize shared etymologies between Hebrew and English.
25. *Protektsiya*, Hebrew for kickback, is of Russian origin.
26. Farmelant invokes and revises Psalm 137:4, "How shall we sing the Lord's song in a strange land?" (KJV), to highlight the speaker's estrangement from and disappointment in Israeli society. This line also alludes to Rachel's poem "*El artsi*" ("To My Country"), which famously opens with the line "I have not sung to you, my country" ("*lo sharti lakh, artsi*"). Whereas Rachel's poem addresses and challenges the value placed on female poetic labor in a time of Hebrew nation-building, Farmelant's poem implies that the State of Israel is no longer deserving of this contribution.
27. Farmelant's final lines revise the optimism and renewal of Song of Songs 2:12, "The flowers appear on the earth; the time of the singing of birds is come, and the voice of the turtle is heard in our land" (KJV).

28. The image of the "aging guest" may allude to the passerby (*'over orach*) in Natan Alterman's *"Od chozer ha-nigun"* ("The Tune Returns"), a poem that appeared in his first collection, *Kokhavim ba-chuts* (*Stars Outside*), published in 1938. In Hebrew, the words *guest* and *passerby* share an etymological root, *a.r.ch,* "to travel." Yigal Schwartz contextualizes the figure of the passerby in modern Hebrew literature in relation to the establishment of the State of Israel: "The passerby is the main persona . . . of the vast majority of literary texts written by the generation of the War of Independence. . . . The passerby is compelled by a preordained, irresistible force: the melody that sets the passerby in motion and presents him with repeated encounters with the wonders of the world. These sights are always surprising and full of youthful and erotic vitality, and the melody is synonymous with this progression." Yigal Schwartz, "The Person, the Path, and the Melody: A Brief History of Identity in Israeli Literature," *Prooftexts* 20, no. 3 (Fall 2000): 318. In Farmelant's poem the looming war cuts short this progression, which the figure of the child/guest embodies.

29. Joshua 1:9, "Have not I commanded thee? Be strong and of a good courage; be not afraid, neither be thou dismayed: for the Lord thy God is with thee whithersoever thou goest" (KJV).

30. These lines contain a reference to the story of Jacob's ladder (Genesis 28).

31. *Tarshish:* A port city that appears several times in the Hebrew Bible, though its exact location remains unclear (2 Chronicles 9:21; 1 Kings 10:22; Jonah 1:3).

32. *Baksheesh:* a tip, bribe, or act of charity (from the Persian for "gift").

33. In Hebrew, *yashan* refers "an old man/thing" but also carries a homophonic association with the verb "to sleep." Isaiah 43:18, "Remember ye not the former things, neither consider the things of old" (KJV).

34. Possibly a reference to Bialik's poem *"Hakhnisini tachat kenafekh"* ("Take Me under Your Wing"), as well as an allusion to Psalm 91.

35. *Ikofez:* from the Greek *egkopeus* (ἐγκοπεύς), "a tool for cutting stone, a chisel" (also appears in Farmelant's poem "Eros" [167]).

36. *Leit man defaleg,* a talmudic expression (Aramaic, "there is no one who differs").

37. See Bialik's early poem *"El ha-aryeh ha-met"* ("To the Departed Lion"), dedicated to the poet Y. L. Gordon (1830–92), one of the key figures of the Haskalah (Jewish Enlightenment).

38. See Kleiman's poem "What Can I Give to You?" (55): "I did not get my fill of learning / and the paths of the world are strange to me. / Only the forefathers' fire is kindled inside me / and I love my people boundlessly."

39. See Bialik's poems *"El ha-aggadah"* ("To the Aggadah") and *"Lifnei aron ha-sfarim"* ("Facing the Library").

40. See Rachel (Bluwstein)'s poem *"El artsi"* ("To My Country") and Psalm 137.

41. Lord Byron's poem "So, we'll go no more a roving" dates to 1817 and was published in the 1830 collection *Letters and Journals of Lord Byron,* edited by Thomas Moore. In my translation, I have corrected the quoted material that appears in the epigraph.

NOTES TO SELECTIONS FROM *FLOWERS OF IDENTITY*

Only the first two lines of Farmelant's poem explicitly translate the first and ninth lines of the English poem, though other lines clearly adapt language and imagery found elsewhere in the original poem.

42. Farmelant's title, "*Shira aviva*," translates into English as "spring poetry." As Shira and Aviva are also common names for girls in Hebrew, I decided to keep the Hebrew title as a nod to the way Farmelant plays linguistically with the daughter-text relation in this poem.

43. *Kulmos*, from the Greek *kalamos*, "a reed pen" (see Farmelant's poem "New Moon"). The Hebrew *kulmos* also refers to the pen used by a *sofer stam*, a Torah scribe.

44. Numbers 16:15, "And Moses was very wroth, and said unto the Lord, Respect not thou (*al tefen*) their offering: I have not taken one ass from them, neither have I hurt one of them" (KJV). In early twentieth-century Hebrew poetry by women (e.g., Rachel [Bluwstein], Anda Pinkerfeld, Esther Raab), we find a number of poems that assert an identification or affiliation with a biblical matriarch. Farmelant's poetry, on the whole, does not follow this trend; instead Farmelant's speakers often articulate a relation to male biblical figures (Kohelet, Job, Jacob, Joshua). In this respect, among others, we can draw a connection between her work and that of Rachel (Bluwstein), whose oeuvre includes a number of poems addressed to or about male biblical protagonists. A notable example is her poem "*Tanakhi patuach be-sefer Iyov*" ("My Bible Is Open to the Book of Job"), which appears in her posthumous collection *Nevo* (1932).

45. Farmelant's poem inverts the imagery of Isaiah 2:4, "And he shall judge among the nations, and shall rebuke many people: and they shall beat their swords into plowshares, and their spears into pruning hooks: nation shall not lift up sword against nation, neither shall they learn war any more" (KJV). This inversion also appears in Joel 3:10, "Beat your plowshares into swords and your pruning hooks into spears: let the weak say, I am strong" (KJV).

46. See note 35 above.

Notes to Selections from *Flowers of Identity*

1. "*Kol dikhfin*," Aramaic, from the Pesach Haggadah: "*Kol dikhfin yeytey ve-yeykhol*" ("All who are hungry come and eat").

2. There is an error in the Hebrew text: in the second line, *lanav* should read as *lagav*.

3. "I tumble about / like a cast-off leaf" (*Hineni na va-vad / ke-'aleh nidach*): In Genesis 4, which relates the murder of Abel by his brother, Cain, God punishes Cain with wandering. "When thou tillest the ground, it shall not henceforth yield unto thee her strength; a fugitive and a vagabond (*na va-nad*) shalt thou be in the earth" (Genesis 4:12; KJV). "*Ke-'aleh nidach*"—"like a cast-off leaf"—is very likely a play on *'aleh nidaf*, a scattered leaf, an expression that appears in Job 13:25, "Wilt thou break a leaf driven to and fro? and wilt thou pursue the dry stubble?" (KJV).

NOTES TO SELECTIONS FROM *FLOWERS OF IDENTITY*

4. In Hebrew the expression *chut shani,* scarlet thread, also denotes a leitmotif. The scarlet thread figures in a pivotal moment in Genesis 38, which recounts the birth of Perez and Zerah, twins born to Tamar and Jacob's son Judah. During labor the midwife ties the scarlet thread around Zerah's hand, which emerges first from the womb, but Perez, whose name means "breach" in Hebrew, is born first (Genesis 38:28). It also appears in Joshua 2:18, "Behold, when we come into the land, thou shalt bind this line of scarlet thread in the window which thou didst let us down by: and thou shalt bring thy father, and thy mother, and thy brethren, and all thy father's household, home unto thee" (KJV); and in Song of Songs 4:3, "thy lips are like a thread of scarlet, and thy speech is comely" (KJV).

5. In this poem and others, Farmelant invokes springtime as an opportunity for renewal but juxtaposes it, in Bialikean fashion, with imagery and suggestions of death and dying. Other poems in this collection that prominently invoke spring include Farmelant's "Shira Aviva," "Everyone Agrees," and "American Trip," as well as Kleiman's poems "Spring," "The Spring," and "Again, Spring."

6. In the Hebrew original, Farmelant's phrase *"niv ha-tefilah,"* which I have translated as "the prayer's idiom," recalls Rachel's poem *"Niv."* In Hebrew, the word *niv* can mean "expression," "idiom," or "dialect," as well as "fang" and "fruit." Rachel's poem rejects the maximalist poetics of her (male) contemporaries and celebrates the modesty and simplicity of her *niv,* or poetic idiom, over the ornamental and densely allusive language that early twentieth-century Hebrew poetry had inherited from the Haskalah, or Jewish Enlightenment. For an overview of the early twentieth-century gender politics of Hebrew poetry in Palestine, see Michael Gluzman's *The Politics of Canonicity: Lines of Resistance in Modernist Hebrew Poetry* (Palo Alto, CA: Stanford University Press, 2003), which includes a close reading of *"Niv."*

7. In Hebrew, *siach* can refer to a bush/plant or conversation. Farmelant is invoking both meanings in this poem, as well as a reference to Genesis 2:5, where the expression *"siach ha-sadeh"* ("every plant of the field") appears.

8. The original contains references to the Jewish prayers *Netz ha-chamah,* "sunrise," and *Ne'ilah,* "locking," the closing prayer of Yom Kippur, which is read in the evening.

9. A reference to the "valley of dry bones" in Ezekiel 37.

10. From the traditional practice of lightly striking the breast while reciting *"Vidui,"* the confessional portion of the Yom Kippur liturgy.

11. According to the Talmudic scholar Marcus Jastrow, the word Farmelant uses, *"sandalkonim,"* may be a corruption of sardonyx but appears to refer more generally to gemstones. To sharpen the contrast between this stone and the *"even mezuyefet"* (false or counterfeit stone) in the following line, I opted to translate *"sandalkonim"* as diamonds. Marcus Jastrow, *A Dictionary of the Targumim, the Talmud Babli and Yerushalmi, and the Midrashic Literature,* vol. 2 (New York: G. P. Putnam's Sons, 1903), 1005.

12. In modern Hebrew, *kikyoni* means "ephemeral," but Farmelant's expression *"tsel kikyoni"* clearly alludes to Jonah 4:6, "And the Lord God prepared a gourd, and made

it to come up over Jonah, that it might be a shadow over his head, to deliver him from his grief. So Jonah was exceeding glad of the gourd" (KJV).

13. In Greek mythology Autolycus is the son of Chione ("snow white") and the god Hermes, from whom he inherited the arts of thievery, trickery, and deception. With these skills he stole Sisyphus's cattle, an exploit that the first century AD Roman author Gaius Julius Hyginus recounts in his *Fabulae*. Farmelant's poem also references Genesis 30, which recounts the story of Jacob and Laban's ("white") speckled flock. The story of Jacob also figures in a crucial speech by Shylock in Shakespeare's *The Merchant of Venice* (act I, scene III). Autolycus is also a character in Shakespeare's *A Winter's Tale*. Line 11, "*ki lavan tsachor*," refers simultaneously to both the biblical Laban and the color white. In Hebrew, Farmelant transliterates the name Autolycus as "*Otoklas*," though the more common transliteration is "*Otolikus*." This discrepancy may be due to a typographical error.

14. This poem appeared in Thomas's 1946 collection *Deaths and Entrances*.

15. Farmelant's phrase "*kos shimurim*" may be an allusion to "*leil shimurim*," the Seder "night of vigil." *Shimurim* also refer to dregs, preserves, or remnants. One of the distinctive features of the narcissus (or daffodil) is its cuplike corona, so it is possible that Farmelant is referring to this characteristic of the flower, though she explicitly doesn't employ any botanical terms. The choice of "watchful" connects my translation to the Narcissus myth and retains a sense of the Seder allusion.

16. Jacques Prévert (1900–1977) was a French poet, screenwriter (of the 1945 film *Les enfants du paradis*, among others), and author of several collections of poetry. Many of his poems, including "L'Orgue de Barbarie" ("The Barrel Organ"), were set to music in his lifetime. L'Orgue de Barbarie, or barrel organ, generally operates by crank and plays music that is encoded into the barrels using pins and staples. In Prévert's poem, the barrel organist kills a group of musicians who talk about playing their instruments more than they actually play.

17. See Uri Zvi Greenberg's poem "*Be-elef ha-shishi*" ("The Sixth Millennium"), in *Eimah gedolah ve-yareach* (*Great Terror and a Moon*, 1925).

18. *Shoah* in Farmelant's Hebrew. Whether or not Farmelant uses the word *shoah* to refer to the Holocaust is unclear in this poem, and by translating it as "catastrophe," I have elected to leave its precise meaning unresolved.

19. See Kleiman's poem "To the Musician" (63).